THEATRE

THEATRE

Richard Foulkes

TEACH YOURSELF BOOKS

For UK order queries: please contact Bookpoint Ltd, 39 Milton Park, Abingdon, Oxon OX14 4TD. Telephone: (44) 01235 400414, Fax: (44) 01235 400454. Lines are open from 9.00–6.00, Monday to Saturday, with a 24-hour message answering service. Email address: orders@bookpoint.co.uk

For U.S.A. and Canada order queries: please contact NTC/Contemporary Publishing, 4255 West Touhy Avenue, Lincolnwood, Illinois 60646–1975, U.S.A. Telephone: (847) 679 5500, Fax: (847) 679 2494.

Long renowned as the authoritative source for self-guided learning – with more than 30 million copies sold worldwide – the *Teach Yourself* series includes over 200 titles in the fields of languages, crafts, hobbies, business and education.

A catalogue entry for this title is available from The British Library.

Library of Congress Catalog Card Number: On file

First published in UK 1999 by Hodder Headline Plc, 338 Euston Road, London, NW1 3BH.

First published in US 1999 by NTC/Contemporary Publishing, 4255 West Touhy Avenue, Lincolnwood (Chicago), Illinois 60646–1975 U.S.A.

The 'Teach Yourself' name and logo are registered trade marks of Hodder & Stoughton Ltd.

Cover photo by David Smith/Eastwing.

Typeset by Transet Limited, Coventry, England.
Printed in Great Britain for Hodder & Stoughton Educational, a division of Hodder Headline Plc, 338 Euston Road, London NW1 3BH by Cox & Wyman Ltd, Reading, Berkshire.

Impression number   10 9 8 7 6 5 4 3 2 1
Year   2002 2001 2000 1999

CONTENTS

PREFACE

In 1962 – on my birthday – I bought a copy of the *Teach Yourself Guidebook to the Drama* by Luis Vargas. Three and a half decades later I was given the opportunity to write this volume in the same series. During the interim I had spent much of my professional life teaching university adult education courses on drama and theatre, so the prospect of producing a book for the general reader was appealing. The first matter to be resolved was the scope of the volume. World theatre was too broad; British theatre too narrow. The solution is a history of the theatre as it developed in Britain with reference to nations which influenced or were influenced by it. This has enabled me to draw in Greece, Rome, Germany, France, Italy, Spain, Norway, Sweden, Russia and the United States at appropriate points in the chronology. I believe that, as a result of this approach, *Teach Yourself Theatre* encompasses the interest range of the typical theatre-goer and student. A particular feature of this work is the inclusion of extracts from contemporary accounts of and about the theatre. These are the timeless raw materials of our study and it is important that readers should have direct access to them. I have, of course, drawn on many works of reference and period-specific histories. I am grateful to the authors and publishers of these, especially those who have given permission for the use of direct quotations. The list of recommended reading provides pointers for those who wish to go into more depth.

I am grateful to Dr Russell Jackson, with whom I have shared an enthusiasm for the Victorian theatre over many years, for being somewhat of a matchmaker between title and author, and to my editor Joanne Osborn, who persisted in finding a way forward with my preliminary proposals.

I recall with appreciation and affection the members of my classes at the University Centre, Northampton during the past quarter-century; I am indebted to them for much of what lies between these covers. I must pay particular tribute to Charles Edwards whose enthusiasm for the theatre has remained undimmed since his schooldays at the College of God's Gift – Dulwich – founded by the actor Edward Alleyn.

I am grateful to Rachel Hayward, who has proved to be a worthy successor to Pat Perkins at the wordprocessor.

I thank my family – whose youngest member, Joel, is no stranger to the jitters and joys of performance – for their support, especially my wife Christine, who has dispensed generous measures of reassurance, encouragement and appreciation during the course of my work on this book.

1 | PRIMITIVE AND CLASSICAL

The will to survive, an instinct for mimicry and a capacity for exuberance are characteristics common to human society through the ages. They also constitute the essentials for theatre in its most elemental form to come into existence.

All primitive societies are preoccupied with the need to survive. This takes three forms: hunting, agriculture and producing offspring.

In the furtherance of these needs communities devise dances linked to the cycle of the year: springtime for sowing, summer for fertilization, autumn for harvest and winter for death. Examples of this initial stage in theatrical evolution have been – and can still be – identified the world over, but in Ancient Greece it gave rise to one of the great periods in the history of drama and theatre.

Dionysus

That the worship of Dionysus in particular, rather than any of the numerous other Greek deities, should result in the birth of drama suggests that he was endowed with uniquely propitious properties. Initially Dionysus's place in the hierarchy was modest. In Homer's time (eighth century BCE) Dionysus was not one of the Olympian deities, but he was worshipped by humbler folk – especially women – to whom his identification with wine and ecstatic dance appealed strongly. During the sixth century BCE Dionysan festivals were established in Corinth, Sicyon, Delphi and Athens and when the Parthenon was completed in the fifth century BCE Dionysus had been accorded his place as one of the 12 Olympians. At Delphi the sanctuary incorporated temples, a sports stadium and a theatre as did the Parthenon in Athens. Worship, sport and theatre were all catered for on the same site.

In contrast to Apollo, who represented reason and restraint, Dionysus (synonymous with Bacchus), having himself been born twice (first from Semele, then from the thigh of Zeus) was associated with the vital force of nature. The cult of Dionysus provided the essentials for drama in all its diversity from the origin of the word tragedy ('Goat-song') to the exaggerated phallus of comedy, but the process must have been a slow one with the decisive point being when **Thespis** of Icaria, the first actor, detached himself from the chorus (50 men), assumed a character (probably by using a mask) and exchanged dialogue with the chorus and its leader.

Not only was Thespis the first actor and probably the inventor of the mask, but c.534 BCE he also won the first tragedy contest which the populist dictator Pisistratus, who had moved the Theatre of Dionysus to that location on the Acropolis where its remains still survive, had included in the expanded Athenian festival known as the Great or City Dionysia. There were three main festivals: the Rural Dionysia, as its title suggests, was observed mainly in the countryside, during the rainy season in December to January; the Lenaea festival, which soon followed in January to February, was devoted to merry-making and more closely associated with comedy than tragedy; but pre-eminent was the City Dionysia held in Athens in April.

The City Dionysia was a major event, 10 months in the planning, attended not only by the citizens of Athens, but by representatives of allied states. It lasted five or six days with assorted processions, games and contests. The drama festival, which occupied the last three days, was in the form of a competition. Dramatists had to submit three tragedies and one satyr-drama (burlesque) – comedy was introduced as a separate category later – and the three finalists were allocated actors, paid for by the state, and a wealthy patron (*choregus*) whose privilege it was to cover the costs of the production. Usually the author himself supervised the staging of his plays.

Nothing remains of the early theatres, which were constructed of wood, but it is possible to establish their principal features. They were – open-air – amphitheatres, usually built on a hillside which provided a natural feature for rows of wooden benches, forming a semi-circle, with a capacity of 15–16,000. The focus of attention was the circular, 19.5 metres (m) (64 feet) diameter, orchestra with its central altar, where the chorus performed. Behind this was erected the *skene*. Initially just a hut, it was gradually expanded into a two-storey building – with at least three entrances – which provided the backscene for most of the locations (temple, palace, house) required by the plays. In due course movable painted scenes were introduced (apparently by Sophocles) to represent non-architectural settings such as the countryside. Whether there was a stage between the *skene* and the orchestra is uncertain, but if there was it can only have been low and narrow. Uncertainty also surrounds the introduction at each extremity (the *paraskenia*) of the *skene*, of *periaktoi*, triangular prisms with each face representing a different place (a tree for the country, etc) which could be rotated as appropriate. Two known, early, features were a cart on wheels upon which a tableau could be arranged and a crane – the *mechane* – (on the upper level of the *skene*) which was used for descents by the gods – hence *deus ex machina*. As for the actors they were equipped with *cothurnus* (a high buskin boot), masks which probably amplified the voice as well as facilitating changes of character and bold costumes – all designed to enhance their impact in such a large theatre.

Such then were the resources at the disposal of the dramatists who created the golden age of Greek drama: Aeschylus, Sophocles and Euripides.

Aeschylus (525–456 BCE)

Born of noble parents Aeschylus, who fought at the battles of Marathon and Salamis, was highly respected as a soldier and citizen as well as a poet. He is reckoned to have written between 80 and 90 plays, of which 79 titles are known, but only seven survive. Aeschylus's three tragedies were usually a linked trilogy – of which the *Oresteia* (458 BCE) is a surviving example – and he won the dramatic contest 19 times. He was responsible for important innovations – reducing the chorus from 50 to 12 and introducing the second actor – which shifted the balance from the lyric to the histrionic.

After his death Aeschylus was accorded the unique distinction that his plays might be revived at the festivals, which were officially restricted to new plays, and that a choregus would be provided for them.

Sophocles (496–406 BCE)

The author of between 90 and 100 plays of which seven survive, Sophocles won 18 victories including one over Aeschylus. His maturity coincided with the prosperity of Periclean Athens; he was elected to important government offices and died – aged 90 – just before the defeat of Athens in the Peloponnesian War. Unlike Aeschylus Sophocles did not write linked trilogies, only completing *Oedipus at Colonus*, a sequel to *Oedipus Rex* (c.425), at the end of his life. Although he increased the chorus from 12 to 15, Sophocles, who introduced the third actor, achieved greater complexity within and between his characters.

Euripides (484–406/7 BCE)

Despite Aristophanes's humorous jibe that his mother was a greengrocer, Euripides came from a good family but, unlike Aeschylus and Sophocles, he did not become involved in the public life of Athens, being something of a recluse. He wrote a similar number (92) of plays to them and more (18) survived, but their unevenness confirms his rather low number of victories (5). In his best work (*Alcestis*, *Ion*) he departed from the strict rules of tragedy to explore human emotions (especially women's) in a realistic way. He introduced the prologue and removed the chorus further from the action – both innovations being influential amongst Renaissance dramatists. In *The Frogs* (405 BCE) Aristophanes stages a contest in Hades between Aeschylus and Euripides with Dionysus as judge to determine which of them should return to earth to revive tragedy.

The Frogs

EURIPIDES: I didn't rave at random, or plunge in and make confusions.
My first appearing character explained, with allusions,
The whole play's pedigree … .
I put things on the stage that come from daily life and business.
Where men could catch me if I tripped; could listen without dizziness
To things they knew and judge my art.

*   *   *   *   *   *   *   *   *   *

DIONYSUS: My tongue hath sworn; – but I'll choose Aeschylus!

translated by **Gilbert Murray** (1886–1957)

Comedy

Of the comic dramatists (Eupolis and Cratinus) of the period **Aristophanes** (c.448–380 BCE) was judged to be the best and it is only his work (11 out of the 40 comedies which he wrote) that has survived. Like tragedy, comedy (*comos*/revel – *ode*/song) had its origins in Dionysan rites, but its development is (even) less clear. The comedy of which Aristophanes was the accomplished exponent was Old Comedy in which a fantastic situation is quickly established and thereafter exploited rather than developed. A dispute takes place about some topical issue, but forthright satire is combined with knockabout farce. The titles of several plays (*Clouds* 423 BCE, *Wasps* 422 BCE, *Birds* 414 BCE) are indicative of the costumes worn by the chorus. Comedies were popular subjects for statuettes and vase paintings in which grotesque and licentious features were prominently depicted.

(a)

(b)

**Greek vase drawings: (a) *comus* performers;
(b) comedy characters**

Old Comedy gave way to Middle Comedy (*The Frogs*) and in due course
to New Comedy of which the most celebrated practitioner was **Menander**
(c.342–292 BCE), but though his reputation had survived, his work had not
until the discovery, in 1905 CE, of a papyrus containing large portions of
three plays. In 1955 CE *Dyskolos* (*The Bad Tempered Man*), originally
produced in 317 BCE, was found, the only one out of his 100 plays to have
survived intact. Menander brought comedy down to earth (rather as
Euripides had tragedy) replacing Aristophanes's flights of fantasy with
observation of contemporary life and skilled characterization. It was from
Menander that the Roman dramatists and their successors derived such
timeless stock characters as the ill-tempered old man, the good-hearted
young rake, the conniving courtesan and the devious slave.

Pros and cons

Although during its years of development and achievement the theatre had
enjoyed state support, wealthy patronage and popular appeal it had not
been without its critics. Within a year of his first victory at the City
Dionysia, Thespis encountered the hostile criticisms of Solon, the
legislator.

Thespis under attack

Thespis, at this time, beginning to act tragedies, and the thing,
because it was new, taking very much with the multitude ... Solon ...
went to see Thespis himself, as the ancient custom was, act and after
the play was done, he addressed him, and asked him if he was not
ashamed to tell so many lies before such a number of people, and
Thespis replying that it was no harm to say or do so in play ...

Plutarch, *The Lives of the Noble Grecians and Romans*, c.46–120 CE

The view that acting, in which one individual pretended to be another, was
inherently a form of lying, and therefore immoral, found a more
sophisticated advocate in the Greek philosopher Plato.

Plato (427–347 BCE)

A disciple of Socrates and Aristotle's teacher Plato occupied and continues
to occupy a vital place in philosophical discourse. Plato's discussion of
poetry is spread through several books of *The Republic*. His objections are

numerous: it is an individual's responsibility to develop his own character and to impersonate others is a departure from that which is liable to involve representing bad characters; imitation, according to Plato's concept of Forms, being a copy of what is already an imperfect copy of the ideal, is 'thrice removed from the King and from the truth'; and the re-enactment of bad behaviour will have an adverse effect on those who see it, who might be tempted to imitate it.

Aristotle (384–322 BCE)

After 20 years as Plato's pupil Aristotle returned to his native Macedonia in 342 BCE as the tutor to Philip of Macedon's son, the future Alexander the Great. That task completed, Aristotle went back to Athens to run the Lyceum where his lectures attracted many scholars. *The Poetics*, generally regarded as a late work, combines in a text which is far from clear, a riposte to Plato, a philosophical account of tragedy and epic poetry, and some evaluation of the work of Sophocles. However, although Aristotle's meaning continues to be disputed, he has been immensely influential, especially following Georgio Valla's 1498 CE Latin translation of *The Poetics*.

Though Aristotle accepted Plato's point that imitative artists would represent good and bad, he asserted that 'the instinct for imitation is inherent in man from his earliest days' as is the pleasure derived by others from the skill with which this is done (Chapter 4). However, rather than leading to the imitation of vice, seeing it 'presented in the form of action, not narration; by means of pity and fear brings about the purgation of such emotions' (Chapter 6). As with so much in *The Poetics* the meaning of this passage is variously interpreted: an ecstatic experience resulting in restored equilibrium; relief that in the end the spectator is released from the tragic hero's fate; a realization that in comparison the spectator's troubles are relatively minor. Whichever interpretation is preferred, catharsis has been undergone.

Other important ideas in *The Poetics* are: the constituent parts of tragedy in order of importance – plot, character, diction, thought, spectacle and song; the unities, though of the three – time, place and action – Aristotle insists only on Unity of Action and commends Unity of Time; and the nature of the tragic hero's/heroine's *hamartia*, the error which, rather than being their own fault (as in the fatal flaw of later tragedy) is inflicted upon them by the gods.

Hellenistic theatre

The surviving theatres of Ancient Greece, like Aristotle's *Poetics* postdate the highwater mark of its drama. In this some observers have detected a pattern: that, though great periods of drama are often followed by extensive theatre building this is not conducive to further high achievements in drama.

During the so-called Hellenistic period – from the death of Alexander in 323 BCE to that of Cleopatra in 31 BCE – theatres were built in every sizeable town in the Greek world. These imposing public buildings were expressions of Greek military, political and cultural power. Stone was the material now used, not only for these new theatres but to replace the old wooden ones. The orchestra – following the disappearance of the chorus – was reduced to a semi-circle but the enlarged stage was as high as 3.65 m (12 feet).

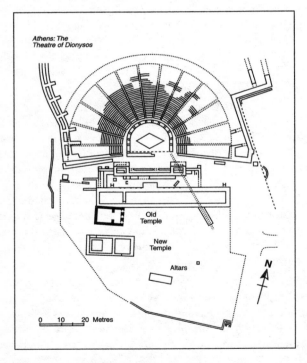

Athens: The Theatre of Dionysos

Old Temple

New Temple

Altars

N

0 10 20 Metres

Plan of the Greek Theatre of Dionysus

The oldest (fifth century BCE) remaining theatre is a small one at Thoricus in Attica; but more impressive and better known are those at Athens and Epidaurus. The Theatre of Dionysus in Athens was reconstructed by the Romans with a semi-circular orchestra, but at Epidaurus on the Peloponnese the magnificent fourth-century BCE theatre designed by Polykleitos the Younger has survived in an excellent state of preservation complete with a full circle orchestra. It now hosts an annual summer festival when its remarkable acoustics enable an actor, using a normal speaking voice, in the orchestra to be heard by members of the audience seated in the top row (of 55), 22.5 m (74 feet) higher.

The Roman way

The origins of Roman drama up to 240 BCE are by no means clear. Literary and archaeological (wall paintings) evidence exists of a theatrical tradition amongst Rome's former rulers, the Etruscans, to the north of Rome in Tuscany and Umbria where some form of satyr drama coincided with, or was derived from, similar developments in Greece at the same time (late sixth century BCE). The Roman historian **Livy**'s (59 BCE–17 CE) account of the introduction of Etruscan dancers to the scenic games in honour of Jupiter in September 364 BCE, when Rome was trying to propitiate the gods during a pestilence, provides a valuable, if somewhat ambiguous, description of a significant event.

Livy's account of the Etruscan dancers in Rome 364 BCE

… when neither human wisdom nor the help of Heaven was found to mitigate the scourges, men gave way to superstitious fears, and, amongst other efforts to disarm the wrath of the gods, are said also to have instituted scenic entertainments. This was a new departure for a warlike people, whose only exhibitions had been those of the circus; but indeed it began in a small way, as most things do, and even so was imported from abroad. Without any singing, without imitating the action of the singers, players who had been brought in from Etruria danced to the strains of the flautist and performed not ungraceful evolutions in the Tuscan fashion. Next the young Romans began to imitate them, at the same time exchanging jests in uncouth verses [*Versus Fescennini*] and bringing these movements into a certain harmony with the words. And so the amusement was adopted, and frequent use kept it alive. The native professional actors were called *histriones* from *ister*, the Tuscan word for player; they no longer – as before – alternatively threw off rude lines hastily improvised, like the Fescennines but performed medleys [*saturae*], full of musical measure, to melodies which were now written out to go with the flute, and with appropriate gesticulation.

translated B.O. Foster, 1924

The key word is *saturae* which is translated as medley or a variety of entertainments, but its meaning has also been traced to 'satyr' opening up the prospect that the Etruscans' entertainment included and introduced the Romans to satyr drama.

Meanwhile south of Rome in *Magna Graecia* Hellenistic culture was established in the form of permanent theatres in which Greek tragedies were performed as were crude farcical dramas, known as *phlyakes*, which are thought to be the subject of illustrations on around 200 vases dating from the fourth century BCE. From this evidence *phlyakes* fell into two categories: those burlesquing the legends and myths which formed the basis of Greek tragedies and those depicting scenes from contemporary life with many of the stock characters (sharp-witted slaves) to be found in later Roman Comedy.

Lucius Livius Andronicus (c.284–204 BCE)

Thus even if, as Livy says, Rome's 'only exhibitions had been those of the circus', the city became subject to powerful influences from the Etruscans in the north and the Hellenistic tradition in the south. The turning-point is precisely identified as 240 BCE when **Lucius Livius Andronicus**, who is said to have been a 'half-Greek' slave from Tarentum in *Magna Graecia*, a city which had the reputation of being obsessed with the theatre, produced in Rome the first Latin version of a Greek play. For the rest of his life Andronicus turned out Latin versions of Greek comedies and tragedies which were performed during the *Ludi Romani* and *Ludi Florales*.

Such evidence as survives (eight play-titles, some fragments, his translation of Homer's *Odyssey* and the judgment of Cicero) suggests that Andronicus chose rather sensational subjects which he handled in a populist way, but his importance as the founder of the main conventions of Roman drama cannot be denied.

Roman holidays

The performance by the Etruscan dancers in 364 BCE had been arranged to placate the gods and as drama took a hold in Rome it was closely linked with religious observance. The festivals (*Ludi Plebeii*) 220 BCE, *Ludi Apollinares* 212 BCE, *Ludi Megalenses* 204 BCE and so on) which proliferated all had a particular religious significance. The responsibility for arranging the – free – programme of events (gladiatorial and animal contests, circuses and so on) fell upon elected officials. A crucial role in the organization of the drama rested with the *Collegium* (guild) of actors and poets, prominent amongst which was **Gnaeus Naevius** c.270– c.199 BCE, who specialized in reworkings of Greek New Comedy. He is particularly renowned for his characterization of the flirtatious courtesan in *The Girl from Tarentum* of which just a fragment survives and the invention of the *fabula praetextata* in which the glories of Rome's past history were depicted. Towards the end of his life Naevius's satirical bent brought him into confrontation with the prominent Metelli family resulting in his imprisonment and exile – a forceful warning of the dangers of offending political and religious power in the city.

Plautus (c.254–c.184 BCE)

Although 21 of his plays have survived, virtually nothing is known about Plautus himself, though he may have come from Sarsina in Umbria. All of his plays were based on Greek (New Comedy) originals including three by Menander. Plautus's own contributions seem to have been: increased verbal humour such as puns; direct address to the audience especially by the cunning slave, a stock character whom he developed considerably, as he did the braggart soldier (*miles gloriosus*); and more convoluted plots.

Shakespeare used the *Menaechmi* as the source for *The Comedy of Errors* with its two sets of twins. Only 300 lines and 42 play titles survive from **Caecilius Statius** (c.219–c.168 BCE) whom both Cicero and Horace rated above Plautus, but he does, however, have another claim on posterity for helping to launch the career of the young Terence with his first play, the *Andria*.

Publius Terence (c.184–159 BCE)

A freed slave from Carthage, Terence mixed with aristocratic and intellectual philhellenists which accounted for the opposition which he encountered from Romans. Although Terence did not consider prologues necessary – a play should explain itself – he wrote one to each of his six plays to reply to the criticisms he had received.

In contrast to Plautus's jokesome buffoonery, Terence exhibited restraint and refinement, improving on his sources, even Menander from whom he departed in the *Andria* to create the first truly romantic comedy.

His humanity, high-mindedness and stylistic distinction secured Terence's place in the library and study (rather than the theatre); in the tenth century CE Hrostvitha studied his plays as models for her own. His work was printed in 1470, two years before Plautus's.

Performance

The plays of Plautus and Terence were originally performed in temporary wooden theatres. Behind the stage was a building with three doors which was suitable for all the locations in the action. The actors wore masks and a company of six was sufficient. Most actors were slaves, but in **Quintus Roscius** (c.120–62) the profession had a leader whose name was to become as permanently associated with it as that of the Greek Thespis. The praise (Cicero), honours and financial rewards heaped upon Roscius during his lifetime were earned by hard work with the actor meticulously preparing every detail of his performance.

Although theatres were still temporary, that built by the *aedile* M. Aemilius Scaurus in Rome in 58 BCE was – from the Elder Pliny's description – a magnificent construction.

Scaurus's theatre in Rome 58 BCE

… just for the temporary use of a few days, Scaurus wrought the greatest work ever achieved by the hands of man … I refer to his theatre. The building had three stories … the lower level was marble, the second glass … and the uppermost … gilded wood … The theatre could accommodate eighty thousand spectators.

Gaius Pliny, *Natural History*

The first stone theatre in Rome was the Theatre of Pompey, which opened in 55 BCE, the inauguration of which Cicero attended and described with its processions – 'six hundred mules' – and spectacle. In 11 BCE Augustus completed the Theatre of Marcellus in Rome which served as a prototype for the theatres which successive emperors built across the empire. The best preserved examples are those at Aspendus in Turkey, Orange in France and Leptis Magna in North Africa.

Vitruvius' *De Architectura*

Between 16 and 13 BCE the Roman engineer **Marcus Vitruvius** wrote his ten books, *De Architectura,* dedicated to the Emperor Augustus. In his fifth book Vitruvius dealt with theatre architecture turning, in Chapter 6, to the *periaktoi.*

Vitruvius on the *periaktoi*

The *scaena* itself displays the following scheme. In the centre are double doors decorated like those of a royal palace. At the right and left are the doors of the guest chambers. Beyond are spaces provided for decoration – places that the Greeks call *periaktoi*, because in these places are triangular pieces of machinery, which revolve each having three decorated faces. When the play is to be changed, or when gods enter to the accompaniment of sudden claps of thunder, these may be revolved and present a face differently decorated. Beyond these places are the projecting wings which afford entrances to the steps, one from the forum, the other from abroad.

translated by Morris Hicky Morgan, 1926

Through Vitruvius, whose work was published in 1486 CE, the Roman theatre became known to and copied by Renaissance practitioners: a free-standing, stone-built theatre, with a small orchestra, a high stage backed by an imposing, richly decorated, facade (*scaenae frons*) the height of which was level with the top of the raked auditorium making it possible to spread an awning right across the theatre. Other features included a curtain which was lowered into a slot in the floor of the stage and perfumed showers to cool and refresh the audience.

The Roman theatre at Verulamium (St Albans) in England, which was built c.150 CE for both religious and secular uses, did not meet such high specifications, but successive reconstructions brought it closer to the conventional Roman theatre. Rediscovered in 1847, it was excavated during 1930–5.

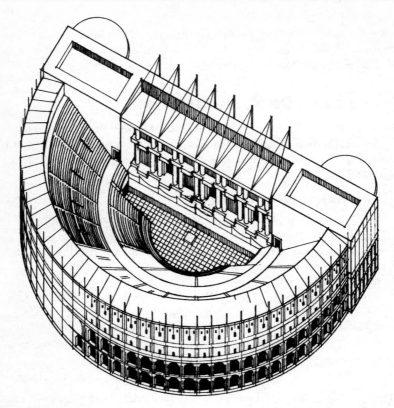

Roman theatre

Nevertheless, the reality was that drama was in decline and the grandiose theatres of the Roman Empire were increasingly occupied by gladiators, wild beasts and pantomimes.

Lucius Annaeus Seneca (c.4 BCE–65 CE)

Ironically it is doubtful whether the Roman Empire's influential dramatist Seneca actually wrote his plays to be performed. A respected orator and stoic philosopher, Seneca was tutor to the young Nero and his adviser as emperor. From the ten plays – which survived in a medieval manuscript – now generally accepted as Seneca's it is clear that he created independent works from his Greek models. His disregard for entrances and exits, the prominence of rhetorical speeches and the apparent impracticality of staging certain scenes suggest that Seneca did not intend his plays to be performed but, nevertheless, with their five-act structure linking chorus and violent climax, they were adopted as a model by many Renaissance dramatists, including Thomas Kyd (*The Spanish Tragedy*, 1586) and Shakespeare (*Titus Andronicus* c.1592–4).

Christian condemnation

During the declining years of the empire the excesses of the theatre brought about a reaction which was strengthened by the advance of Christianity culminating in its adoption as the official religion in 330 CE. The Christian case against the theatre had already been advanced by **Tatian** c.160 CE and **Tertullian**.

Tertullian: *De Spectaculis/Of Public Shows* 198 CE

The Theatre is especially the shrine of Venus ... The very harlots also, the victims of lust, are brought forward on the stage ... The very community of feeling, their very agreement or disagreement in party-spirit, doth by their intercourse, fan the sparks of carnal lust ...

translated by the Reverend Charles Dodgson, 1842

In the fourth and fifth centuries regional church councils withdrew the sacrament from actors and imposed the penalty of excommunication – by implication eternal damnation. In his *Confessions*, **St Augustine** 354–430 CE admitted and renounced his youthful enthusiasm for the stage in Carthage. In 533 CE in Rome and 692 CE in Constantinople the theatrical spectacle ceased.

2 | THE MIDDLE AGES

It is important to remember the duration of the period generally known as the Middle Ages: it stretched from the fall of the Western Roman Empire in the fifth century CE to the Renaissance in the fifteenth. In terms of the British theatre, therefore, the Middle Ages cover a spectrum from the final flickers of Roman theatre to the early glints of the glories of the Tudor stage. Other parts of Europe both paralleled and diverged from developments in England.

Roman remains

The last contemporary reference to the Roman stage in Western Europe is a letter dated 533 CE, but in Constantinople and the Eastern Empire the theatre survived somewhat longer with records of performances as late as 692. In the eyes of some of its most virulent critics the depraved state of the theatre had been at least a factor in the fall of the once great empire.

The theatres so imperiously erected throughout the subject territories from Carthage to Caerlion, though falling into dereliction, remained massive reminders of a former occupation. By the end of the fourth century the Roman theatre at Verulamium (St Albans) was reduced to a rubbish dump, but in France the theatres at Nimes, Arles and Orange were occasionally used and it has been suggested that the ancient Roman tradition may explain the 'rounds' in which the Cornish Mysteries and some other medieval dramas were performed.

More significant than the survival of Roman theatre buildings was the triumph of Latin as the universal language of the Church and post-imperial Europe. Complete command of the language involved reading classical authors and ecclesiastical libraries contained works by Aristotle and the Greek dramatists – translated into Latin – alongside Seneca, Terence and Horace.

Hrotsvitha of Gandersheim (c.935–73)

Hrotsvitha or Roswitha was a German noblewoman – not a nun – living with a Benedictine order in Gandersheim, Saxony. She wrote six plays *Abraham*, *Callimachus*, *Dulcitius*, *Gallicanus*, *Pafuntius* and *Sapientia*. Hrotsvitha's subject matter was Christian, but it was Terence who provided the model for her dramas, though she may not have written them with performance in mind. Nevertheless, Hrotsvitha's plays are important examples of the survival of classical influence in the Middle Ages.

Written at about the same time, the *Passion of Christ* incorporates, bodily, several hundred lines out of Euripides's plays including passages preserved nowhere else. Significant though this evidence of the survival of ancient drama was for dramatists of the Renaissance, there is no escaping the almost total independence of medieval religious drama from classical influence.

Mummers and minstrels

Though the Church had succeeded in suppressing the theatre the impulse to entertain and to be entertained was irrepressible.

The earliest forms of performance, which of course pre-dated Christianity, were associated with the cycle of the agricultural year – the winter solstice on 23 December, the summer solstice on 23 June, the vernal equinox on 15 March and the autumnal equinox on 15 September. Ploughing, shearing sheep, harvesting and slaughtering cattle were high points of this cycle which reflected humanity's basic preoccupation with fertility, growth and survival. Not surprisingly the Christian Church simply adopted these existing festivals for its own calendar.

Pope Gregory to Saint Augustine in 601

Where of old they were wont to sacrifice cattle to demons, thither let them continue to resort on the day of the Saint to whom the Church is dedicated and slay their beasts no longer as a sacrifice, but for a social meal in honour of him whom they now worship.

Though not recorded until the eighteenth century mumming plays constitute arguably the earliest form of vernacular drama. Thus of the most celebrated example Richard Southern wrote: 'Again, a corruption in Hanoverian times has made the hero in some versions, King George. We go back to find that earlier he is *Saint* George. But is this, then, a Christian rite? Surely – no. Presumably a more primitive, pre-Christian hero lies still deeper, hidden by the polite imposition of Saint George.' (*The Seven Ages of the Theatre*, p.45) With its phallic emblems (blades), its duels in which one or other combatant is killed only to be resuscitated by the doctor, the St George play expresses the ritual of death and rebirth which is by no means limited to the Christian festival of Christmas.

Though the agricultural/religious cycle provided set points for established festivals, there were other occasions for entertainment. Family events such as a birth, baptism or marriage provided the opportunity for the village as a whole to enjoy a performance of songs and tales by a minstrel. Over the centuries demand and supply grew. When Margaret of England married John of Brabant in 1290, 426 minstrels were present. Schools and guilds of minstrels were formed in France (1321). Where minstrels went jesters, ballad-mongers, jugglers and acrobats followed. Though the noted minstrel **Rahere** (d. 1144) apparently advanced from King Henry's jester to Prebendary of St Paul's Cathedral and founder of St Bartholomew's Hospital, entertainers were not generally welcomed by Church authorities.

Thomas de Chabham, Sub-Dean of Salisbury Cathedral (d. 1313)

There are three kinds of *histriones*. Some transform and transfigure their bodies with indecent dance and gesture, now indecently unclothing themselves, now putting on horrible masks. There are besides others who have no definitive profession, but act as vagabonds, not having any certain domicile, these frequent the Courts of the great and say scandalous and shameful things concerning those who are not present so as to delight the rest ... There is yet a third class of *histriones* who play musical instruments for the delectation of men, and of these there are two types. Some frequent public drinking-places and lascivious gatherings and sing there stanzas to move men to lasciviousness. Besides these there are others, who are called *jongleurs* who sing of the gestes of princes and lives of the Saints.

Quem quaeritis?

By the time Thomas de Chabham wrote his attack on the 'three kinds of histriones' the most significant development in the evolution of medieval drama had taken place in a church. The introduction of the '*Quem quaeritis?*' into 'The Proper' (the part of the mass used only for a particular festival, as opposed to 'The Ordinary' which was used throughout the year) for the third nocturn at matins on Easter morning had been amongst the various elaborations of the liturgy developed by Benedictines on the continent during the ninth and tenth centuries. The text was delivered as an antiphon between a single cantor and a group of responders.

> *Quem quaeritis in sepulchro, O Christolae?*
> Whom do you seek in the sepulchre, O Christian women?
>
> *Jesum Nazarenum crucifixum, o caelicola*
> Jesus of Nazareth who was crucified, O heavenly one.
>
> *Non est hic: surrexit sicut praedixerat.*
> *Ite, nuntiate: quia surrexit de sepulchro.*
> He is not here: He has risen even as he foretold.
> Go announce that He is arisen from the sepulchre.

Shortly afterwards another *troped introit*, in which the shepherds ask the angel where they may find the infant Jesus, was added to the Proper for Christmas Day.

Glynne Wickham has pointed out that these additions – sung in Latin – were integral to the liturgy, rather than either a scripture lesson or an entertainment: 'whatever else this stanza was for its pioneers it was never conceived or regarded as some sort of visual aid to Bible reading for the education of illiterate peasants ... – but as a new dimension to the depth of emotional response to the event commemorated and thus as an enhancement of faith in its abiding significance.' (*The Medieval Theatre*, p.37)

The promptness and precision with which Ethelwold, Bishop of Winchester issued the *Concordia Regularis* (c.970) demonstrated the Church's determination both to exploit and control what had evidently become a favoured development of its liturgy for the two major festivals of Easter Sunday and Christmas Day. Though his purpose was undoubtedly religious, Bishop Ethelwold showed a strong sense of the dramatic potential of the liturgy and a sure ability to exploit it.

Concordia Regularis

While the third lesson is being chanted, let four brethren vest themselves. Let one of these, vested in an alb ... approach the sepulchre without attracting attention and sit there quietly with a palm in his hand. While the third response is chanted, let the remaining three follow ... vested in copes, bearing in their hands thuribles with incense, and stepping delicately as those who seek something approach the sepulchre. These things are done in imitation of the angel sitting in the monument and the women with spices coming to anoint the body of Jesus. When therefore he who sits there beholds the three approach him like folk lost and seeking something, let him begin in a dulcet voice of medium pitch to sing *Quem quaeritis* [and so on through the dialogue already quoted] And ... let him [priest as Angel] lift the veil, and show them the place bare of the cross ...

Chanted Latin and priests dressed in copes representing women, Bishop Ethelwold's directions combined artificial, formal, ornate religious ritual and the essentials (dialogue, mystery) of drama culminating in the participation of the congregation/audience in the shared climax of thanksgiving with the *Te Deum* and bell-ringing.

Corpus Christi

In 1264 Pope Urban IV announced the new feast day of Corpus Christi, which was eventually instituted by his successor Clement V in 1311 and by 1318 was widely observed throughout Europe.

The fact that the Papacy instituted an additional feast day, for which there was no specific reference in the Church calendar, so close to Whitsun and therefore the longest day (and the best hope for good weather) certainly lends force to Peter Happé's view that 'there seems to have been something very deliberate about the establishment of the feast which may have led to the concentration of dramatic episodes on that day.' (*English Mystery Plays*, p. 19)

Corpus Christi Day being the Thursday after Trinity Sunday is a movable feast, depending on the date of Easter, but it must fall within the period 21 May–24 June – close to the summer solstice, which before the reformation of the calendar fell ten days earlier. Though some scriptural sequences (*Le jeu d'Adam* and *Creation* and *Passion* performed by the clerks of London) pre-date its creation, the Feast of Corpus Christi undoubtedly had the effect of stimulating the widespread and vigorous growth of popular religious theatre. The long-held view that the Church expelled an increasingly popular, secular and unruly activity into the streets and squares hardly seem to be tenable. More likely the Church recognized the advantages of extending its influence by collaborating with the trade guilds to produce more ambitious representations which would divert the people from the unsavoury entertainments about which Thomas de Chabham protested.

Mystery plays

Cycles of mystery plays based on The Bible were performed across Europe. Four English cycles survive:

YORK – 48 plays
CHESTER – 24 plays
TOWNELEY (actually WAKEFIELD) – 32 plays
LUDUS CONVENTRIAE (an unidentified town, probably in the
East Midlands) – 42 plays

Single plays exist from Norwich, Northampton and Newcastle-upon-Tyne and two plays from Coventry and Brome (Suffolk). Records show that cycles were performed in Aberdeen, Bath, Beverley (a full list), Bristol, Canterbury, Dublin, Ipswich, Leicester, Worcester and possibly Lincoln and London. As Peter Happé has demonstrated there is a remarkable consistency in the 'episodes' included in the four extant cycles and the Beverley list.

Episodes

The Fall of Lucifer
The Creation and Fall of Man
Cain and Abel
Noah and the Flood
Abraham and Isaac
Moses (not Beverley)
The Prophets (not Beverley; Balaam at Chester)
The Nativity – Annunciation, Suspicion of Joseph, Shepherds,
    Purification, Magi, Flight into Egypt, Massacre of the Innocents
The Baptism (not Chester)
The Temptation (not Towneley)
Lazarus

The Passion – Conspiracy, Judas, Last Supper, Caiaphas,
   Condemnation, Crucifixion, Lament of Mary, Death
The Resurrection and Ascension
The Assumption and Coronation of the Virgin (not Towneley)
Doomsday

English Mystery Plays, p.25

An important notion is that of correspondences between a story from the Old Testament and one from the New (for instance the death of Abel and sacrifice of Isaac foreshadowing the crucifixion) to illustrate the prevailing theme of Christ's sacrifice and the redemption of man.

The authors of the plays remain unidentified. With the plays being performed annually over a period of 200 years there were recurrent revisions and frequent borrowings. The single play in which the greatest authorial talents and inventiveness are evident is *The Second Shepherds' Play* from the Wakefield cycle in which the story of the nativity is combined with a pseudo-nativity involving a stolen sheep. Four more plays and parts of others are attributed to the Wakefield Master.

The dramatic text remained the preserve of the Church, which had the authority to commission new plays and change, or cut, existing ones; but the staging of these plays was largely entrusted to the craft guilds with support from the city or town councils.

Mounting the stage

Allardyce Nicoll identified six forms of theatre:

1 the church as theatre
2 the church-like arrangement of the acting-place when the
   first drama was brought to the open air
3 the stationary setting
4 the pageant
5 the round
6 the curtained platform.
   (*The Development of the Theatre*, p.64)

In England the usual form was the pageant.

Archdeacon Robert Rogers of Chester (d. 1595)

Every company had his pagiant or parte, which pagiants weare a
high scafolde with two rowmes, a higher and a lower, upon four
wheeles. In the lower they apparelled them selves, and in the higher
rowme they played, being all open on the tope, that all behoulders
mighte heare and see them. The places where they played them was
in every streete. They began first at the abay gates, and when the
firste pagiante was played it was wheeled to the highe crosse before
the mayor, and so to every streete.

English medieval wagon stage

The pageant wagons were purpose-built vehicles which were carefully
stored in their own pageant houses (garages) for the rest of the year. Meg
Twycross (*The Cambridge Companion to Medieval English Theatre*, p.47)
has calculated the size of these wagons as 2.45 m (8 feet) wide by
3.05–4.27 m (10–14 feet) long, with the stage floor 1.22–1.53 m (4–5 feet)

above street level and the roof 2.45 m (8 feet) above that. Acting space was restricted, though there is evidence that the action sometimes spilt on to the street as in the Coventry Shearmen and Taylors' Play: 'Here Erode ragis in the pagond and in the strete also'.

Modern revivals of the cycles especially in Chester (1983) and York (1988 and 1992) have added to our understanding of the original staging. Tony Harrison's version of the York cycle – *The Mysteries* – performed by the National Theatre, London between 1977 and 1985 also contributed significantly to the growing appreciation of medieval drama.

The actors

The cramped conditions on the pageant wagons would not have permitted the presence of the clerical master of ceremonies, who is evident in both visual and written records of continental productions such as that at Valenciennes where a large stationary stage was used. Even when the pageant master ceased to be a clergyman the Church would nevertheless have had a say in his appointment. Rehearsals, in England usually held early in the day before work began, took place from Easter onwards. The final 'general rehearse' (dress rehearsal) was attended by the committee of management and leading benefactors. Though images of Bottom and the other Mechanicals in Shakespeare's *A Midsummer Night's Dream* are not inappropriate, it must be remembered that many actors performed the same role year after year and that each year they performed the same play several (12–16) times. Repetition was the order of the day.

The style of acting is the subject of considerable speculation. Clearly there was little scope for character identification (in York 22 different actors played Christ during the same performance), the goal was to communicate the religious material; a powerful voice was essential. For this reason, if no other, women did not usually take part, though in the Chester play of the *Assumption* the Virgin was allocated to 'The wives of the town'.

With some actors – inevitably – more successful than others an element of rivalry and professionalism developed. Records show payments ranging from a few pence to several shillings. The scale was based on dramatic rather than religious importance: God could get as little as 6d (2.5p); Herod (a star-role in the making) as much as 4s. 6d (22.5p).

Scenery

The major expenditure was on the scenic aspects of the production. Plays were often performed by guilds who possessed a particularly appropriate skill – the Waterleaders and Drawers of Dee for the Chester *Noah* for instance. As Philip Butterworth has shown, immense resources of materials, money and skill were expended upon fire effects; 'blazing swords, burning altars, flaming devils, dragons and hell-mouth' (*Theatre of Fire Special Effects in Early English and Scottish Theatre*).

The Mouth of Hell is a particularly prominent feature in Hubert Cailleau's miniature of the Valenciennes Mystery Play (1547). Fire was not cheap as the London *Drapers' Repertory* for 1541 reveals: '3s. 8d for a gallon of "aqua vitae" to burn in the dragon's mouth, 16d to him that kept fire in the dragon's mouth'.

Mouth of Hell from the Valenciennes Mystery Play (1547)

The reckoning

The escalating costs of staging the great Mystery Cycles were met by special levies – 'Pageant-silver', 'Pageant-pence'. By 1501 the average cost of each pageant staged by the City of London for the reception of Catherine of Aragon was 120 pounds. As Glynne Wickham concludes: 'they [the Mystery Cycles] collapsed and disappeared because the economics of play-production on so lavish and extended a scale had become too unwieldy for performances to continue without strong management at the centre' (*The Medieval Theatre*, p.89).

Another crucial factor was the Reformation consequent upon Henry VIII's divorce from his wife upon whose welcome so much pageantry had been expended. The last-recorded performances in England were at York (1569), Chester (1575) and Coventry (1580); but a similar fate overtook the Mystery Cycles in Catholic France where they were suppressed by an enactment of the Parliament de Paris in 1548.

Miracle plays

The earliest known example of a Saints (Miracle) play is that of St Katharine at Dunstable in the early twelfth century. These plays, celebrating a particular saint, tended to be local, but though by the fifteenth century they were more widespread, in England they never attained the number and variety which they did in France.

Morality drama

Excepting the fragmentary *Pride of Life*, the earliest Morality to have survived is *The Castle of Perseverence*, usually dated 1400–25. Running to 3,700 lines the play focuses on the progression from birth to death of a simple, representative, man (mankind) who encounters such allegorical figures as the seven deadly sins and the seven virtues. Compared with the Mystery Cycles this and other Morality plays (*Everyman* for instance) are simplified, concentrated and close-knit.

The stage diagram which survives in *The Castle of Perseverence* manuscript has given rise to much speculation and, though it indicates some sophistication with the scaffolds for the three enemies of mankind (the World, the Flesh and the Devil), it suggests far less elaborate stagecraft than required by the Mystery Cycles. It was undoubtedly a far less expensive undertaking.

Whether it was toured by professional actors or produced by local groups, *The Castle of Perseverence* was not specific to a particular place and would certainly have suited St Just-in-Penwith and Perranporth where the Cornish Passion Play (*Ordinalia*) was presumably performed. *The Castle of Perseverence* was, in fact, revived at Perranporth in 1969. Of earlier performances in Cornwall **Richard Carew** provided a vivid account.

Richard Carew, *Survey of Cornwall*, 1602

The quasy miracle, in English, a miracle play, is a kinde of interlude, compiled in Cornish out of some scripture history ... For representing it, they raise an earthen amphitheatre in some green field, having the diameter of this enclosed playne some 40 or 50 foot. The country people flock from all sides, many miles off, to delight as well the eye as the eare; the players conne not their parts without booke, but are prompted by one called the Ordinary, who followeth at their back with the book in his hand and telleth them softly what they must pronounce aloud.

Interludes

As the final theatrical form of the Middle Ages, Interludes provide an important bridge to the Tudor period. The origin of the name is obscure and may be derived from interludes in lengthy Mystery or Morality plays or intervals at banquets. In style, Interludes are still allegorical, but with considerable comedy and farce. They are short and the verse is usually doggerel. A notable example of the Interlude is **John Heywood**'s (c.1497–1580) *The Four Ps* (published 1545) in which a Pedlar judges between a Palmer, a Pardoner and a 'Pothecary as to which is the greatest liar, the prize going to the Palmer who says that he 'never saw or never knew any woman out of patience'. Their dramatic style aside the Interludes are significant because they were performed indoors (at Court, in noblemen's houses, Inns of Courts and Colleges) by professional actors. The casts were small, the scenic requirements modest.

During the Middle Ages the theatre had progressed from being suppressed by the Church to being embraced by it and then outgrowing it. The great Mystery Cycles clearly represent one of the high points of popular theatre in which the majority of the locality's population was involved either as a participant or onlooker.

The trend – driven as much by economic and social forces as by artistic ones – was towards professionalism: a small number of performers staging a less elaborate entertainment to a more selective audience.

3 | AROUND THE GLOBE

Henry VII, who became King of England in 1485 following his defeat of Richard III, maintained a company of four actors with John English at their head. Each of the King's two sons had his own troupe: Prince Arthur by 1498, Prince Henry by 1506. Many noblemen, such as the Earls of Oxford, Northumberland and Derby, supported private companies. Henry VIII doubled the size of his father's company to eight and Queen Elizabeth I (the last Tudor monarch; d. 1603) expanded it to 12. However, it would be a mistake to assume that these monarchs wished to share their enthusiasm for theatre with their subjects at large. Such was definitely not the case.

Unfriendly acts

With Henry VIII's assumption of the title Supreme Head of the Church of England in 1535, his realm's separation from the Roman Catholic Church was complete. The first decree with implications for theatrical activity was that of 1537 abolishing the majority of annual festival days ('the number of holy days is so excessively grown') and leaving only four (Christmas Day, Easter Day and the Feasts of St John the Baptist – midsummer – and St Michael) for general observance. The Act of 1543 endorsed 'plaies and interludes ... for the rebuking and reproaching of vices, and the setting foorth of vertue', but in 1545 the City of London's 'Proclamation for the Abolishment of Interludes' applied the earlier legislation to repress theatrical activity within its bounds. The proclamation identified attendance at plays with the provocation 'to all proclyvyte and Redynes of dyvers and sondrye kyndes of vyce and synne', with youths in particular, neglecting their work and worship. The performance 'of any maner of Enterlude or common playe' was henceforth banned within the City of London with only a few exemptions – 'the houses of gentlemen ... in the open stretes ... as in tyme past ... in the commen halles of the Companye's felowshipps or brotherheddes of the same citie'.

Under Edward VI additional Acts (the Act of Uniformity imposed penalties for irreligious matter) and Proclamations (28 April 1551 requiring professional theatre companies to be licensed) placed further restrictions on the theatre, which Queen Mary reaffirmed, though her motive was to curb anti-Catholic pieces such as those by **John Bale** (1495–1563) author of *Kynge Johan* (1538). The accession of Queen Elizabeth in 1558 provided no relief to the players.

Queen Elizabeth's Proclamation, 16 May 1559

The Quenes maiestie doth straightly forbyd al manor of Interludes to be playde, eyther openly or privately, except the same be noticed before hande, and licenced within any citie or towne corporate by the Maior or other chiefe officers of the same, and within any shyre, by such as shalbe Lieuetenauntes of the Quenes Maiestie in the same shyre, or by two of the Justices of peax within the part of the shire where any shalbe played.

An Acte for the Punishment of Vacaboundes, and for the Relief of the Poore and Impotent, Statute 14, 1572

Common Players in Enterludes and Minstrel, not belonging to any Baron of this Realme or towardes any other honorable Personage of greater Degree; mynstrels juglers, ... shall wander abroade and have not Lycence of two Justices of the Peace at the least ... shalbee taken adjudged and deemed Roges Vacaboundes and Sturdy Beggars.

Peter Thomson describes this as – in hindsight – 'a charter for the establishment of a professional theatre in England'. (*Shakespeare's Professional Career*, p.44) Certainly its effect was to suppress casual performances and for (the better) actors to seek the security of patronage. In 1574 the Queen granted a patent to the Earl of Leicester's Company first mentioned as Leicester's Men in 1559. One of their number was James Burbage.

Pedagogues and prodigies

The professional theatre's halting progress was not dependent upon the rediscovery of the surviving works of the Ancient dramatists. That process was having more effect in institutions of learning in which the performance of plays was accommodated alongside instruction in oratory and rhetoric.

Nicholas Udall (1505–56)

Following his own education at Winchester and Corpus Christi College, Oxford, Udall became successively Headmaster of Eton College and Westminster School. A scholar of repute, Udall put his knowledge of Plautus and Terence to good effect in writing robust comedies with broadly drawn characters to be performed by his pupils. Though the exact date of Udall's *Ralph Roister Doister* (no earlier than 1534, no later than 1553) is not known, it is generally regarded as the first English comedy.

Gorboduc

The palm for the first English tragedy is usually awarded to *Gorboduc*, the joint work of **Thomas Norton** (1532–84) and **Thomas Sackville** (1536–1608), who was both a scholar and a nobleman. The play, which was acted at the Inner Temple Hall on Twelfth Night 1561, combines a classical structure (based on Seneca) with a national subject (Gorboduc, King of Britain ill-advisedly dividing his realm between his two sons).

A distinction has to be made between plays such as Udall's being performed by pupils at prestigious schools and the so-called boy companies (Hamlet's 'little Eyases'). Though the origins of the boy companies may go back to the fourteenth century their formative period was the mid sixteenth century when Sebastian Westcott was Master of the choristers of St Paul's Cathedral and Richard Edwardes of the Chapel Royal. The exact whereabouts of the playhouse within the precincts of St Paul's remains uncertain, but the Blackfriars Theatre in part of the Blackfriars monastery is more fully documented. It opened in 1576 – its prime mover being Richard Farrant, Deputy Master of the Children at the Chapel Royal – with dimensions of 14 m by 8 m (46.5 feet by 26 feet); its capacity was about 100.

Following Farrrant's death in 1580 the two companies merged under John Lyly.

John Lyly (c.1553–1606)

A noted courtier and alumnum of Oxford and Cambridge Lyly, through his prose romance *Euphues* (1578) added the word 'euphuism' to the English language. A gifted stylist, well versed in classical mythology and the principles of rhetoric, Lyly wrote his plays with the talents of the companies and the sophistication of their audiences in mind. *Campaspe* and *Sappho and Phao* (both 1584) were successful, but Lyly's intervention in the Martin Marprelate controversy through a satirical pamphlet (1589) and his use of the company to publicize this led to the suppression of their performances. After a silence of ten years the boy companies enjoyed great success during the opening decade of the seventeenth century.

An expanding city

Their unfortunate embroilment in religious controversy notwithstanding the indoor theatres of the boy companies could not accommodate either the volume or the taste of London's burgeoning population, estimates of which vary from 60,000 in 1520, to 100,000 in 1560, to between 160,000 and 220,000 by the early seventeenth century.

The demand for entertainment in what was an, increasingly, entrepreneurial city inevitably increased. The larger inns, such as The Boar's Head, with their galleried courtyards were well suited to performing plays. Prior to 1574 there were two animal-baiting rings in London, thereafter until 1603 the Bear Garden was permitted to stage plays on Sundays when the theatres were closed. Richard Leacroft is confident that 'it is unlikely that the unroofed theatres built at this time were consciously based on the circular plan of the Roman theatre, the shape being undoubtedly derived from bull and bear baiting yards'. (*The Development of the English Playhouse*, p.29).

Although, given the attitude of the authorities to the theatre, the attractions of adaptable and multi-functional structures were considerable, the financial incentives to erect a theatre became irresistible. The first to succumb appears to have been John Brayne at his property the Redd Lyon in Whitechapel in 1567, but it is to his brother-in-law James Burbage that the credit for constructing the first purpose-built theatre is usually given.

The Theatre, 1576

In view of the City of London's 'Proclamation for the Abolition of Interludes' (1545) Burbage sited the Theatre beyond the city walls, north of Bishopsgate along Shoreditch.

Burbage acquired a lease of 21 years on the land and his total outlay amounted to the considerable sum of £700. In the absence of detailed evidence, the assumption is that the Theatre was polygonal with three galleries and a stage surmounted by some sort of upper structure. The fact that, on the expiry of his lease, Burbage had the Theatre dismantled and used the materials for the construction of the Globe suggests that he, prudently, kept his investment as flexible as possible.

The Theatre was undoubtedly a risky venture. Burbage had to contend with the opposition of the City and the Church; the vicissitudes of the weather and the perils of the plague. From the point of view of climate the summer was the best time to perform, but if deaths by plague reached 40 a week (1577, 1578 and 1581 were bad years) the theatres and baiting-yards were shut and the players were forced to tour in the provinces or venture abroad, as one unidentified troupe did to Elsinore in 1585. With artisans earning 6s (30p), a week the 1d (0.04p) charged for admission to the pit was far from prohibitive even if the extra 1d (0.04p) for a seat was. A further 1d (0.04p) ensured not only a position of greater comfort but the attention of other members of the audience. With an estimated capacity of 3,000, the proceeds from a full house were considerable.

The Burbage family

James Burbage (c.1530–97), a joiner by trade, acted with the Earl of Leicester's men and built the first theatre. He took over and rebuilt the Blackfriars Theatre in London in 1596, but died before he was allowed to re-open it.

Cuthbert Burbage (c.1566–1636), inherited the Theatre and was responsible for the construction (using some of the Theatre timber) of the Globe, 1599.

Richard Burbage (c.1567–1619) was the greatest actor of his day. He probably began his career with the Admiral's Men at the Theatre; he was the first to perform Shakespeare's Richard III, Hamlet, King Lear and Othello.

The Lord Chamberlain's Men

During its early years the Theatre was not the exclusive preserve of any particular company, but in 1594, following closure for a severe outbreak of plague, it was occupied by the Lord Chamberlain's Men, so called because their patron Lord Hunsdon was the Lord Chamberlain. Through his influence the company gained access to the Court, giving 13 of the 20 royal commands between 1594 and 1597. The rival Admiral's Men gave the other seven. Originally (1576–9) known as Lord Howard's company they changed their name to the Admiral's Men on his appointment as Admiral in 1585. The major beneficiaries of the Lord Chamberlain's Men's success were its share-holders who at the outset were: Cuthbert and Richard Burbage, Thomas Pope, Augustine Philips, John Heminge, William Kempe and William Shakespeare.

Theatres

Success breeds imitation and long before the occupancy by the Lord Chamberlain's Men, the Theatre faced competition. **The Curtain**, which opened in 1577 on a site close to the Theatre, though it survived until c.1627, was never a prominent playhouse. Neither was **Newington Butts** for which references exist from 1580 to 1594. **The Rose** c.1587 to 1605 in which Philip Henslowe held the major stake stood on the south bank of the River Thames on a site, the excavation of which in 1988–9 provided valuable archaeological evidence about the Elizabethan playhouse.

The Swan, c.1596, the property of Francis Langley, also on the south bank, was the subject of a famous account and drawing by a Dutch traveller Johannes de Witt who described its 'wooden columns painted in such excellent imitation of marble', built on 'a mass of flint stone' and accommodating 'in its seats three thousand persons'.

The Globe was built on Bankside by Cuthbert Burbage in 1599 using materials from the Theatre. Of all Elizabethan theatres it is the subject of the most intense speculation, being the theatre with which Shakespeare was most closely associated. It was burnt down during a performance of *King Henry VIII* on 29 June 1613. The more elaborate second Globe was erected on the same site in 1614 and survived until 1644. Sam Wanamaker's plan to rebuild Shakespeare's Globe was finally realized in 1997 (see Mulryne and Shewring *Shakespeare's Globe Rebuilt*).

The Fortune was built for Philip Henslowe in 1600 in Cripplegate in the Liberty of Finsbury, north of the city boundary. The Fortune contract survives showing that, unlike other contemporary theatres, it was square. The Fortune contract is at its most tantalizing in its recurrent references to the Globe Theatre, as in 'And the saide stadge to be in all other

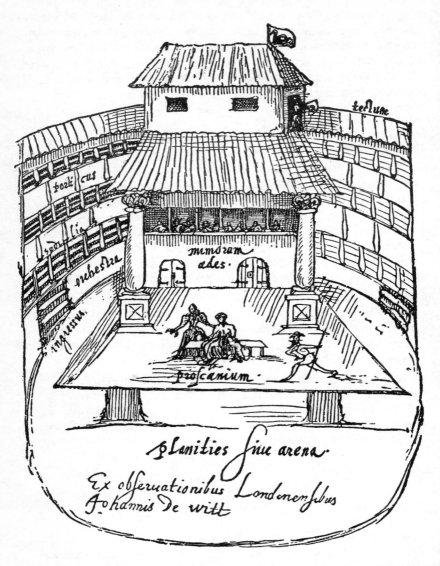

A copy of a drawing by Johannes de Witt of the Swan Theatre, c.1596

proporcions contryved and fashioned like unto the Stadge of the saide Plaie Howse called the Globe'. The stage was 13 m (43 feet) wide and extended 6.5 m (22 feet) into the middle of the yard. Edward Alleyn and the Admiral's Men were closely associated with the Fortune. Burnt down in 1621 it was rebuilt in brick, finally being demolished in 1661.

Philip Henslowe (c.1550–1616)

Unlike most other theatre managers, Henslowe never worked as an actor; he was essentially an entrepreneur. He had been apprenticed to a dyer and his subsequent business interests included manufacturing starch, mining, pawnbroking, money-lending and property as well as the theatre. Over the years Henslowe's theatrical empire included the Rose, possibly a share in Newington Butts, the Fortune and the Hope.

Henslowe's family life reinforced his business connections. He married the wealthy widow of the dyer to whom he had been apprenticed and her daughter Joan married the actor Edward Alleyn in 1592. In 1619 Alleyn founded Dulwich College (originally the College and Hospital of God's Gift) where Henslowe's papers were deposited and remain to this day.

Henslowe's *Diary*, as it is usually called, is a (arguably the) major documentary source for the Elizabethan theatre. In it Henslowe recorded daily receipts, payments to playwrights and actors, inventories of costumes and much else besides. Henslowe did not charge the companies, of which the Admiral's Men led by Alleyn was the most significant, a fixed rent, but covered some of their expenses and claimed a (high) proportion of the daily takings.

The Red Bull was an inn used for plays prior to its conversion to a theatre in 1605. Situated in St John Street, Clerkenwell, it was probably square.

The Hope belonged to Henslowe and Alleyn for whom it was erected close to the Swan in 1614. Conceived for both plays and animal baiting it seems to have become increasingly reliant on the latter; it survived until 1656.

Thirty-seven years separate the construction of the Theatre and the Hope, a long-enough period for significant changes to take place in playhouse design and construction. The Bankside emerged as the favoured location. Mulryne and Shewring have characterized the area as a 'bustling unfashionable locality; and the site of activities of which modern residents might not be entirely proud', but that no doubt added to the excitement of crossing the Thames by boat or over London Bridge and escaping the jurisdiction of the narrow-minded City of London authorities. Though the more fanciful accounts of the Mermaid Tavern have now been discredited, there is no doubt that the Bankside was conducive to the creation of what Mulryne and Shewring describe as 'a noteworthy artistic community' (*Shakespeare's Globe Rebuilt* p.18).

The Museum of London's archaeological excavations in 1989, which uncovered 60 per cent of the Rose and 10 per cent of the Globe, revealed unexpected features. The Rose was significantly smaller with a diameter of about 20 m (66 feet) compared with around 30.5 m (100 feet) at the Globe. Its floor was covered in masses of crushed hazelnut shells and, more significantly, there was a 1 in 10 incline, a rake from the gallery walls down to the centre. This led to speculation as to whether other theatres incorporated the same feature. Professor Thomson took the view that they most likely did; Professor Gurr pointed to the lack of proof. Another issue was the conflicting evidence about the location of the stage, which after extensive research has been positioned at the south end of the yard at the reconstructed Globe so that the afternoon sun shines, not on the players, but the occupants of the galleries.

Archaeology has provided valuable new evidence to be assessed alongside existing documentary material such as de Witt's account and drawing, Hollar's long view of London, Visscher's *Panorama*, the Fortune contract and the plays themselves. The task of producing a template of the Elizabethan outdoor theatre is as fraught as ever, but the main features were: a yard – possibly raked; an encircling structure with three galleries; a raised platform stage with a trap door; two entrance doors in the back wall possibly with a recess between them; an upper stage suitable for balcony scenes; an overhanging canopy with some flying equipment.

Audiences

Clearly the flurry of theatre building was based on the premise that there was substantial demand waiting to be satisfied. Thomas Platter, a visitor from Basel in 1599 gives a vivid impression of Londoners at the theatre: 'Every day at two o'clock in the afternoon in the City of London two and sometimes three comedies are performed, at separate places, wherewith folk make merry together, and whichever does best gets the greatest audience.'

To attend the theatre was, in the eyes of its critics, to expose oneself to many perils: sickness, theft, the company of 'vagrant persons, maisterles men, thieves, horse stealers, whoremongers, Coozeners, Conycatchers, Contrivers of treason, and other idele and daungerous persons' and the content of the plays themselves which was likely to 'drawe the same into imitacion and not to the avoidinge the like vices which they represent' (Letter to the Privy Council from the Lord Major and Alderman of the City of London protesting against the Swan Theatre, 1597). At risk was not just mortal well-being, but the prospect of heaven in the afterlife.

Who were those intrepid Elizabethans who, despite these dire warnings, ventured inside these alluring buildings which were clearly amongst the largest and most impressive in the capital?

Over the years scholars exploring this subject have come up with different answers. Alfred Harbage in *Shakespeare's Audience* (1941) characterized the audience at the open-air theatres as socially diverse, but with the artisans to the fore. As her title – *The Privileged Playgoers of Shakespeare's London* (1981) – implies, Ann Jennalie Cook found the better educated and affluent in the ascendance. Andrew Gurr in *Playgoing in Shakespeare's London* argues that, to some extent, each theatre had its own clientele. The playhouses north of the city were favoured by a coarser, less discriminating audience and, even on the Bankside, the Globe attracted a better-informed following than the Rose. The question of attendance by women (or more specifically respectable citizens' wives) is particularly pertinent. Gurr observes; 'Ladies went relatively rarely to the common playhouses before 1600, but were in numbers at the Globe from 1599 to 1614, and became a major section of the audience at the indoor venues by Caroline times.' (p.64)

Playwrights

The demand for new plays was voracious. It has been likened to Hollywood in the 1930s, but television might be an apter comparison with the total audience being catered for in one showing and (perhaps) a repeat. Andrew Gurr gives the repertoire of the Admiral's Men at the Rose during the 1594–5 season as an example. Performing six days a week they presented 38 plays, of which 21 were new, introduced at more or less fortnightly intervals. Two of the new plays were performed only once, and only eight survived through to the following season.' (*The Shakespearean Stage 1574–1642*, p.103). In 1595–6, 19 new plays were performed and in

1596–7, 14. Of the most popular plays Marlowe's *Tamburlaine I* achieved 14 performances and *Tamburlaine II* 6 performances during 1594–5.

A playwright would probably begin by interesting the manager in his ideas, hopefully secure a down-payment and set about completing the script as rapidly as possible. He would need to take account of the facilities, features and limitations of the theatre for which he was writing and ensure that there were parts for all the actors in the company. It has been calculated that in his early plays Shakespeare provided six major roles (with over 200 lines). For the rest doubling would have been extensive. Many plays were collaborative with two, three or even more writers contributing the type of material at which they were most adept. **Samuel Rowley** (c.1575–1624) is credited with a hand in many plays including *The Taming of a Shrew* and providing Henslowe with additional comic passages for Marlowe's *Dr Faustus* in 1602.

Christopher Marlowe (1564–93)

Born in Canterbury, the son of a shoe-maker, Marlowe went to Corpus Christi College, Cambridge becoming a BA in 1584 and, after some delay, an MA in 1587. Homosexual, atheist and secret agent, Marlowe met his end in a Deptford tavern in circumstances which will probably never be fully explained.

Though he died before he was 30, Marlowe left a rich legacy. His plays *Tamburlaine I* (1587), *Tamburlaine II* (1588), *Dr Faustus* (1589), *The Jew of Malta* (c.1590) and *Edward II* (1591–2) provided the Admiral's Men with a string of successes at the Rose and Edward Alleyn with leading roles which he exploited to the full. Not only did Marlowe's plays enjoy sustained popularity, but with his mastery of blank verse and his characterization of defiant aspiration he set the pace for his contemporaries and successors.

Thomas Kyd (1558–94)

A friend of Marlowe with whom he was implicated in accusations of heresy, in extricating himself from which Kyd shifted attention to his fellow dramatist. Although the lost *Hamlet* (Shakespeare's source) has been ascribed to Kyd, his reputation rests on *The Spanish Tragedy* (c.1585), which long remained one of the most popular plays in the repertoire of the Admiral's Men and had, by 1633, passed through ten printed editions to serve as the prototype for a succession of revenge tragedies.

Thomas Heywood (1573–1641)

By his own count Heywood had a hand in 220 plays, most of which are lost. Of his prolific output (for the Admiral's Men and Worcester's Men) the most enduring is *A Woman Killed with Kindness* (1603) in which he displays psychological insight and emotional power. Much of his other work – written at speed for money – is lax, with both plot(s) and poetry declining in power.

William Shakespeare (1564–1616)

Born in Stratford-upon-Avon where he attended the Grammar School, Shakespeare sought his fortune in London where he became actor, shareholder and dramatist. Shakespeare contributed at least 36 plays to the theatre, of which 16 were printed in quarto editions during his lifetime. His collected plays appeared in the First Folio of 1623 prepared by John Heminge and Henry Condell, his former colleagues, with Ben Jonson's ringing eulogy;

> … Soule of the Age!
> The applause! delight! the wonder of our stage!

It was with the Lord Chamberlain's Men, initially at the Theatre and subsequently at the Globe and Blackfriars that Shakespeare was long associated and for whom he wrote most of his plays. He also found favour at Court and the Inns of Court.

Though it was in London that Shakespeare achieved fame and wealth, he retired to his home town, in which he had acquired extensive property, where he died and was buried. Of the multitudinous biographical volumes on Shakespeare, *William Shakespeare A Compact Documentary Life* by S. Schoenbaum is recommended.

Ben Jonson (1572–1637)

The posthumous son of a clergyman, Jonson was a promising classical scholar under Camden at Westminster School, but he lacked the means to attend university and earned his living in various occupations before joining a troupe of strolling players.

Henslowe's *Diary* records Jonson as both an actor and playwright in 1597 when he may have been one of the authors of the controversial (lost) play *The Isle of Dogs* at the Swan Theatre. The next year Jonson escaped hanging for killing a fellow actor by pleading benefit of clergy and wrote his first comedy *Every Man in His Humour*. Jonson's range was impressive: *Cynthia's Revels* (1600) for Blackfriars, the tragedy *Sejanus* (1603), his most enduring comedies *Volpone* (1606) and *The Alchemist* (1610), and – in collaboration with Inigo Jones – the masques, which will be considered in Chapter 4. Though he fell on hard times, Jonson exercised significant influence during his lifetime and beyond.

The author's manuscript of a play was known as the 'foul papers'; there would also be 'parts' for the actors and the book-keeper's (prompt) copy. A summary of the plot would be displayed for the benefit of the company. Unusually Shakespeare evidently retained ownership of his early plays which formed part of his investment in the Lord Chamberlain's Men, but a play became the property of the company which had bought it. Even allowing for the high failure rate – which obviously did not apply to Shakespeare – the repertoire gradually expanded and the demand for new plays eased off. Canny as ever, Henslowe often paid a hack playwright a pittance to revise some dated piece.

The financial rewards for playwriting were modest compared with those for acting and, more markedly, theatre management. Shakespeare's fortune was derived from his share in the Lord Chamberlain's Men rather than his acumen with the quill.

The players

The style of Elizabethan acting has been the subject of many theories. Hamlet's advice to 'the Players' has been upheld as a blueprint.

HAMLET: Speak the speech, I pray you, as I pronounc'd it to you trippingly on the tongue, but if you mouth it, as many of our players do, I had as lief the town-crier spoke my lines … Be not too tame neither, but let your own discretion be your tutor. Suit the action to the word, the word to the action; with this special observance, that you o'erstep not the modesty of nature …

Shakespeare, *Hamlet*, Act 3, Scene 2

Against this has been set the more formal model of oratory and rhetoric as detailed by John Bulwer in *Chirologia, or the Naturall Language of the Hand* (1644).

In his account of the working conditions of Elizabethan actors, Peter Thomson stresses that the actor's most important skills were 'external' (*Shakespeare's Professional Career*, p.92): dancing, fencing, singing and above all holding the audience's attention. The scope for characterization, let alone interpretation, would have been slight with each actor being supplied with just his own 'part'/'parts' (with cues) and only about 12 mornings 'to complete the learning, making, costuming and rehearsing' of a play (p.88). The key to success was that the actors were used to working together and could get a play up to performance standard very quickly ... as weekly repertory companies did in the mid-twentieth century and television 'soap operas' continue to do, producing several episodes every week.

It has been estimated that 80 per cent of the scenes which Shakespeare wrote for the Globe could be performed on a bare stage. With scenery kept to a minimum – a few basic props and essential pieces of furniture – the stage remained uncluttered, free of hampering impedimenta and their

Boy-actor Nathan Field in female costume in Kyd's *The Spanish Tragedy*

accompanying hazards. As Henslowe's *Diary* shows, more money and attention was expended on costumes: a 'black velvet cloak with sleeves embroidered all with silver and gold' cost a staggering £20-10s-6d (£20.53).

In an all-male company wigs were particularly important. The boy actors in the open-air theatres belonged to a tradition different from their counterparts in the 'boy-troupes' being bound as apprentices and sometimes continuing in their female roles up to their late teens (or even beyond). Some of them became full members of the company and even share-holders.

Nathan Field (1587–1620)

The son of an anti-theatrical cleric, Field was a scholar at St Paul's School, London, where he was impressed into the company of boy actors. An immediate success, he moved to the Blackfriars where he appeared in several plays by Ben Jonson, who took charge of his education. In 1613 Field joined the – adult – Lady Elizabeth's Men, transferring two years later to the King's Men. Handsome, talented – he wrote two plays – and dissolute, Field was often in debt and fathered an illegitimate son by the Countess of Argyll.

During a period of rapid development and contrasting venues, acting styles inevitably varied and developed. What was appropriate for *Tamburlaine* at the Rose would have been out of place for a more mature Shakespeare play, especially indoors. The trend was away from bombast and declamation towards greater subtlety.

'those that play your clowns'

In his advice to the Players, Hamlet enjoins 'those that play your clowns [to] speak no more than is set down for them'; later he recalls Yorick, his father's jester, as 'a fellow of infinite jest, of most excellent fancy' (Act 5, Scene 1). In both cases it is thought likely that Shakespeare had **Richard Tarleton** (d.1588) in mind. Tarleton was particularly renowned for the jig and though he belonged to acting companies (Queen Elizabeth's Men, 1583) he was more of an extempore performer than an actor ... hence Hamlet's strictures.

Another contender for Hamlet's advice was **Will Kempe** (d.1603), who was also a noted exponent of the jig. Additionally he was a share-holder and popular actor in the Lord Chamberlain's Company where he is known to have played Dogberry (*Much Ado About Nothing*) and probably played Bottom (*A Midsummer Night's Dream*) and Launcelot Gobbo (*The Merchant of Venice*). Whether Kempe's tendency to speak more than was set down for him accounted for his departure from the company in 1599 is uncertain, but he was certainly unabashed and generated massive publicity by dancing from London to Norwich.

Robert Armin's (c.1568–1615) assumption of Kempe's place as the leading clown in the Lord Chamberlain's Company is thought to have brought about Shakespeare's shift from broad comedy (Bottom, Dogberry) to the wise fool (Feste in *Twelfth Night*, Lear's Fool) in a more reflective vein.

Leading men

The two leading actors of the period were Edward Alleyn and Richard Burbage. Portraits of both men (Burbage's possibly a self-portrait) hang in the gallery at Dulwich College.

Edward Alleyn (1566–1626)

The son of an innkeeper, Alleyn soon achieved prominence with the Admiral's Men at the Rose where he created the leading roles (Tamburlaine, Faustus and Barabas) in Marlowe's plays. His marriage to Henslowe's step-daughter Joan Woodward in 1592 consolidated his position and before the end of the decade he retired from the stage to pursue his business interests. Alleyn resumed acting at the newly opened Fortune Theatre in 1600, but his declamatory style had become dated and he finally retired around 1604. He built and endowed Dulwich College and was able to settle £1,500 on his second wife, the daughter of John Donne. Alleyn demonstrated that the theatre could be profitable and respectable.

Richard Burbage (c.1567–1619)

Though he began his career in Alleyn's (Strange's/Admiral's) company, Burbage achieved his reputation as the leading man in the Lord Chamberlain's/King's Company at the Theatre/Globe and Blackfriars. His range as an actor was remarkable, encompassing Shakespeare's Richard III,

Hamlet, Lear and Othello and Ferdinand in Webster's *The Duchess of Malfi*. His style was judged to be true to life. The inheritor, with his brother Cuthbert, of the Globe and share-holder in the Lord Chamberlain's Company, Burbage, unlike Alleyn, resisted the lures of commerce and remained an actor. He left a modest estate (£300) to his widow, but his enduring testimonial is as the first great English actor:

Epitaph on Richard Burbage

Hee's gone and with him what a world are dead
Which he revivd, to be revived soe.
No more young Hamlett, ould Heironymoe.
Kind Leer, the greued Moore, and more beside,
That lived in him, have now for ever dy'de.
Oft have I seen him leap into the grave
Suiting the person which he seem'd to have
Of a sadd lover with soe true an eye,
That theer I would have sworn, he meant to dye.
Oft have I seene him play this part in jeast
Soe lively, that spectators, and the rest
Of his sad crew, whilst he but seem'd to bleed,
Amazed, thought even then he dyed in deed.

The concurrence of remarkable individuals and a tide of events to which they are ideally suited produces the greatest achievements of humankind, sometimes in the face of measures (banning play-acting in the City of London) which turn out to stimulate what they were intended to suppress.

4 | NEW PERSPECTIVES

During the sixteenth century English actors ventured as far as Elsinore in Denmark and, in 1611, a company of English comedians visited Poland with Shakespeare's plays. The traffic was by no means one way. Probably the most widely travelled and influential troupe was the Gelosi from Italy who were popular performers in London and Paris during the latter years of the sixteenth century. Their leading lady was **Isabella Andreini** (1562–1604) who excelled as the young girl in love (the *innamorata*) in the *commedia dell'arte* which formed an important part of the Gelosi repertoire.

Commedia dell'arte

Commedia dell'arte ('Comedy of the Profession') sprang up in northern Italy during the second half of the sixteenth century. The essence of *commedia dell'arte* is improvisation with actors creating their own dialogue – within the scenario outlined by the manager – for the masked stock characters of which Arlecchino (Harlequin), Colombina (Columbine) and Pantalone (Punch) were the most celebrated. The origins of *commedia dell'arte* are obscure. Though similarities with Roman mime and the comedies of Plautus and Terence have been noted it is not possible to trace direct descent. What is certain is the widespread influence of *commedia dell'arte*. **Ben Jonson** (1572–1637) in England; **Lope de Vega** (1562–1635) in Spain; **Molière** (1622–73) and **Marivaux** (1688–1763) in France and **Goldoni** (1707–93) in Italy.

Latin/Italian

The rediscovery and imitation of Roman drama predated, and may indirectly have given rise to, *commedia dell'arte*. By 1450 there were groups staging Roman drama and imitations in Latin in Rome (under

Pomponius Laetus), Ferrara, Florence, Siena, Venice and Naples. Printing provided another means of promoting classical authors with editions of Terence appearing in 1493 – Lyons – and 1497 – Venice – with both of them providing evidence of contemporary staging. Of the new generation of dramatists writing in Italian, rather than Latin, **Niccolo Machiavelli** (1469–1527), **Pietro Aretino** (1492–1556) and **Ludovico Ariosto** were the most successful.

Ludovico Ariosto (1474–1533)

Best known for *Orlando Furioso*, an epic of chivalry, Ariosto, who was courtier, administrator and poet at the ducal court in Ferrara, wrote four stage comedies in the Roman vein. *Lena* (*La Lena*) is the most notable for its combination of subtle characterization and realistic background. It was the basis for **George Gascoigne**'s (c.1525–77) *Suppositi* (*Supposes*), the first extant English prose comedy, originally performed at Gray's Inn in 1566.

Vitruvius (c.70–15 BCE)

Marcus Pollio Vitruvius was a not particularly distinguished architect, working in Rome during the principate of Augustus Caesar, (first century BCE), whose *De Architectura Libri Decem* provided posterity with the only architectural treatise to survive from ancient times. Although known earlier in other copies, the official date for the rediscovery of Vitruvius's manuscript is 1416. The first printed edition edited by Leone-Baptista Alberti was published in Florence in 1484. Other editions followed: 1511 by Fra Giocondo (Jocundus), reprinted six times between 1513 and 1535; 1521 by Caesar Caesariano; 1556 by Danielo Barbaro. Barbaro's edition of Vitruvius was a collaborative work with the architect Andrea Palladio and, unlike previous editors, they examined surviving remains of Roman theatres and made use of their findings.

Andrea Palladio (1508–80)

Born in Vicenza, Palladio attempted to revive the dignity and severity of Roman architecture, drawing on Vitruvius. His own *I quattro libri dell'Architettura* was published in 1570 and was immediately translated into most European languages. Palladio's style and that of his students became known as Palladian of which Inigo Jones was a noted exponent in England.

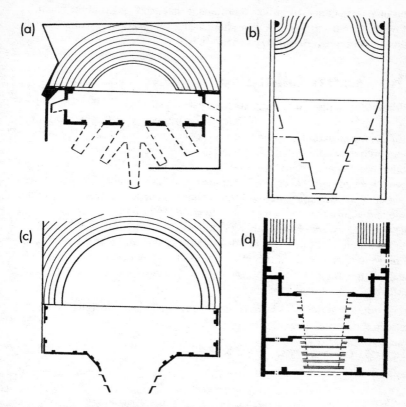

The evolution of the stage from (a) Vicenza to (b) Sabionetta, (c) Inigo Jones and (d) Parma

Vicenza

The city of Vicenza in the north Italian region of Veneto was the location of a sequence of significant developments in theatre building. In the 1530s Sebastiano Serlio built a temporary theatre on the Roman circular model in the courtyard of the Palazzo Porto. The Accademia Olimpica, which was founded as a society for the study of antiquity and the production of classical and pseudo-classical drama, commissioned Palladio, who was one of its members, to build a permanent theatre. Construction began in May 1580, but Palladio died in August and the work was completed in 1584 by **Vincenzo Scamozzi**, (1552–1616).

The Teatro Olimpico

Although designed according to the best classical principles, the Teatro Olimpico incorporated several interesting innovations: the auditorium is elliptic; the structure is roofed. In accordance with the classical plan there is an orchestra between the stage and the lowest row of seats. The wooden stage, painted as marble, is a long narrow rectangle, 25 by 7 m (82 by 22 feet), backed with a richly ornamented scenic facade (*scaena frons*) pierced with five apertures: a large central arch, lesser arches on either side and a doorway in each of the side walls. In Palladio's original design the apertures were closed either by doors or backcloths, but Scamozzi, in step with current theatrical trends, added permanent perspective 'vistas' representing streets running into the courtyard which is the stage. The scale of the Teatro Olimpico was huge with a capacity of 3,000. It is still extant.

In introducing the perspective vistas into Palladio's designs Scamozzi reflected the influence of Sebastiano Serlio.

Sebastiano Serlio (1475–1554)

Born in Bologna, Serlio worked in Rome and Paris where the second book of his *Regole generali di Architettura* (*General Rules of Architecture*) was published in 1545. This volume (one of seven) dealt with perspective painting on the stage. The stage platform, 18 by 3 m (58 by 10 feet), was backed by a rear, raked, scenic stage where changeable backcloths, flanked by flats, painted in perspective were located. Serlio provided three standardized settings:

The Comic Scene

This first shall be comicall, whereas the houses
must be slight for citizens, but specially there
must not want a brawthell or bawdy house,
and a great Inne, and a Church …

Serlio's perspective scene for tragedy

The Tragic Scene

Therefore in such cases you must make none but stately
houses ... I have made all my scenes of laths, covered
with linnen, yet sometime it is necessary to make some things rising
or bossing out; which are to be made of wood ...

The Satyric Scene

The Satiricall Scenes are to represent Satirs, wherein you must place all those things that bee rude and rusticall ... for which cause Vitruvius speaking of Scenes, saith, they should be made with Trees, Rootes, Herbs, Hils and Flowres, and with some country houses ...

Serlio's writing on the theatre was published in English in 1611 and by 1620 had been translated into four other languages. His influence was immense, establishing the convention – of the (three-dimensional) actor performing against, not in, the painted, illusionistic setting – which was to prevail for centuries to come.

Serlio's ideas made the Teatro Olimpico something of an anachronism from the outset and subsequent theatres developed in different ways. When Scamozzi designed the Teatro di Sabionetta for the court of Vespasian Gonzago in 1588 he retained the decorative style of Palladio but widened what now could be recognized as a proscenium arch to accommodate Serlian-style scenery. Similarly, Aleotti's Teatro Farnese at Parma (1618–19) dispensed with the fixed archways for side-wings and a backcloth.

Inigo Jones (1573–1652)

The son of a London, Roman Catholic clothworker, Jones was appointed to Prince Henry's household in 1604 and thereafter, until the outbreak of the English Civil War, supervised the majority of Court masques. Prior to his royal appointment Jones had been in the Earl of Rutland's embassy to Denmark to present the Order of the Garter to King Christian IV, brother of Queen Anne. Other early travels, if they occurred, went unrecorded. In 1609 Jones visited France, including the ancient theatre at Orange. In 1613–14, initially as part of the Earl of Arundel's embassy accompanying the Princess Elizabeth and the Elector of Palatine after their wedding in London, Jones travelled through Strasbourg, Basle, Milan, Venice, Parma, Vicenza, Rome, Genoa and Turin. He annotated a copy of Palladio with notes about the buildings he visited; described the Teatro Olimpico at Vicenza; met Scamozzi and acquired a large quantity of Palladio's architectural designs. By then Jones had created a reputation which went before him, but even in his early work there is evidence of his wide reading on Italian architecture.

The masque

The masque (French spelling having supplanted the English, mask) had origins in primitive religious rites and folk ceremonies but, though its essence remained, the arrival of guests in disguise, bearing presents and joining in a dance with their hosts, the occasions became more diverse and the appurtenances (scenery, machinery, costumes, speeches) increasingly elaborate. The masque was the court entertainment of James I and Charles I with members of the royal family appearing in these, hugely expensive, productions in which the combined talents of Ben Jonson and Inigo Jones, who worked together between 1605 and 1634, were frequently displayed. Other accomplished writers of masques were **Thomas Campion** (1567–1620), **George Chapman** (c.1560–1634) and **Samuel Daniel** (c.1563–1619). The first Jonson and Jones collaboration, costing up to £3,000, was *The Masque of Blackness* in which the six-months pregnant Queen Anne appeared, at her own express wish, black faced (as did her ladies).

Although the ladies had supposedly journeyed to the court so that they could be turned white by the king's power, the traditional transformation back to their real (white) selves was obviously beyond the power of stagecraft.

The significance of the king's presence, if not participation, was underlined by the attention paid to 'the level of the state': 'The vanishing point of the perspective was at the level of the King's throne ("the state") – he alone viewed from the perfect position' (David Lindley ed. *Court Masques*, p.216).

The Masque of Blackness

The Queen's masques: the first
Of Blackness

Personated at the Court at Whitehall,
on the Twelfth Night, 1605 ...

Oceanus, presented in a human form, the colour of his flesh blue ...

Niger, in form and colour of an Ethiop ...

The masquers were placed in a great concave shell, like a mother of pearl, curiously made to move in those waters, and rise with the billow ...

These thus presented, the scene behind seemed a vast sea (and united with this that flowed forth) from the termination or horizon of which (being the level of the state, which was placed in the upper end of the hall) was drawn, by the lines of perspective, the whole work, shooting downwards from the eye; which decorum made it more conspicuous and caught the eye afar off with a wandering beauty. To which was added an obscure and cloudy night piece, that made the whole set off. So much for the bodily part, which was of Master Inigo Jones his design and act ...

Ben Jonson

Christ Church, Oxford

In August 1605 King James I attended the Act, the annual week of ceremonies consisting of debates, feasts and dramatic entertainments held by the University of Oxford. The plays were the responsibility of the university, but the Court provided carpenters of the King's Works from Whitehall under their Comptroller, Simon Basil to construct a theatrical auditorium, a drawing of which survives in the British Library. In John Orrell's judgement 'The indication that it shows the hall at Christ Church lies in one of the written comments "The hall is a 115 foote longe and 40 broade ..." No hall in England other than Christ Church possessed such dimensions ...' (*The Theatres of Inigo Jones and John Webb*, p.26).

The plan shows the auditorium, for which Basil was responsible, and as for *The Masque of Blackness*, the King's vantage point was a major consideration as a visitor from Cambridge recorded:

'the art perspective'

They (the Earls of Worcester, Suffolk and Northampton) utterlie disliked the stage at Christchurch, and above all, the place appointed for the chayre of estate because yt was no higher ... much troubled the *Vice chancelor*, and all the Workmen, yet stood in defence of the thinge done, and maynteyned that by the art perspective the kinge should behould all better then if he sat higher.

The plan gives only a hint of the Inigo Jones staging ('a flat forestage with a steeply raked and presumably scenic stage beyond it'. *The Theatres of Inigo Jones and John Webb*, p.26) and the Cambridge observer's report lacks clarity, but Isaac Wake is more informative.

Isaac Wake

The scene occupied the upper part of the hall; its stage (*Proscenium*) running down to a level part in a gentle incline, which lent great dignity to the entrance of the players, as if descending a hill ... The cloths and houses of the scene were skilfully changed by means of a machine time and again according to all necessary places and occasions ... not only from day to day for each production, but even in the course of a single performance.

The sloping stage and the moving clouds, which Wake goes on to mention, correspond with Serlio's perspective theatre, but the machines capable of changing scenery before the audience's eyes belong to a different tradition. Orrell traces them to Vitruvius, a copy of which in Danielo Barbaro's edition with Palladio's illustration of the triangular *periaktoi* Inigo Jones possessed, and identifies this as the first use of this kind of *scena versatilis* on a major English stage. How the *periaktoi* rotated on a raked stage and how the vista at the back of the stage was changed in unison with the *periaktoi* remains unresolved, but it is evident that at Christ Church for the performances of the satyr play *Alba* (27 August), the tragedy *Ajax Flagellifer* (28 August) and the comedy *Vertumnus* (29 August), with the addition of Samuel Daniels' *Arcadie Reformed* as a treat for the Queen and Prince Henry on the last day, Jones created scenery for the three types (tragedy, comedy and satyr) of classical drama in which he combined the traditions of Vitruvius and Serlio.

Appropriately it was in Oxford 60 years later that **Christopher Wren** (1632–1723) brought the classical tradition of theatrical architecture to life in the Sheldonian Theatre (1664–7). The Sheldonian was constructed for the annual Act ceremonies – the Encaenia – (conferring of degrees) so its features do not correspond exactly with those of conventional theatre. It is D-shaped with two galleries, the woodwork is treated as stone in the Roman manner but, though the classical influence is undeniable, John Orrell considers that Wren drew almost as much inspiration from the small Cockpit Theatre in Drury Lane.

The Cockpit in Drury Lane

Far from being an original theatre design the Cockpit, as its name implies, was the outcome of adaptation. Just as the outdoor London theatres owed some of their features to bear-baiting, so did the Cockpit to cock-fighting.

The Cockpit, 15 m (50 feet) square, was erected for its original purpose in 1609 by John Best. In 1616 Best leased the building to Christopher Beeston, who set about converting it into a small indoor theatre for Queen Anne's Men, already a popular attraction at the Red Bull. There was considerable opposition to Beeston's development and that he was able to complete it was thanks to a proclamation by James I which stipulated that new buildings must be constructed in brick or stone on existing foundations. A proclamation of 12 October 1607 permitted such buildings to exceed the original foundations by one third.

In 1974 Iain Macintosh identified a set of drawings (in the Jones/Webb collection at Worcester College, Oxford), which had previously been regarded as 'a proposed design rather than an executed structure' (Leacroft, *The Development of the English Playhouse*, p.73), with Beeston's Cockpit Theatre. These drawings show a U-shaped auditorium and a rectangular stage – consistent with the former being half the original Cockpit and the latter being an addition within (or probably just over) the permitted limit. Jones evidently based two of the drawings on Palladio's designs for the Teatro Olimpico in Vicenza, which he had visited; the auditorium is classical in style; the stage is backed by an architectural *trans scenae* with three openings, the centre one being an arch with a Serlian vista, the other two simply doors.

John Orrell's verdict on the Inigo Jones plans – the Cockpit Theatre – is: 'For all the humanistic quality of its method of design, the Cockpit remained essentially a Jacobean playhouse best suited to the poetic, non-scenic drama of the age.' (*The Theatres of Inigo Jones and John Webb*, p.60)

Although it was vandalized by rowdy apprentices on Shrove Tuesday 1617 the Cockpit was quickly rebuilt (as the Phoenix). Following the closure of the theatres in 1642 illicit performances still took place resulting in a raid by Commonwealth soldiers in 1649. However, William Davenant, who had succeeded **William Beeston** (c.1606–82), Christopher's son, in 1640, was granted licences to stage two plays with music (early operas), *The Cruelty of the Spaniards in Peru* (1658) and *Sir Francis Drake* (1659), which paved the way for a resumption of regular activities after the Restoration of the Monarchy in 1660. The last recorded performances were in 1665.

Another theatre with which Inigo Jones's designs have been linked was the Salisbury Court Theatre which opened in 1630.

The Cockpit-in-Court

Whether or not the Cockpit in Drury Lane spurred Charles I to commission Jones, as Surveyor General of the King's Works, to convert the Cockpit-in-Court into a theatre in 1629–30, that structure had a long and most illustrious history. The Court Cockpit had been erected at Whitehall for Henry VIII c.1530–2 and had been refitted for Queen Elizabeth I in 1581–2. During James I's reign plays were occasionally performed in the Cockpit, but an extensive re-modelling of the space was required to convert it into a theatre. Evidence is supplied by the Works account and some drawings by John Webb (at Worcester College) which, although they probably arise from the 1660 refitting, provide vital information about Jones's design. The stage, 11 m (36 feet) wide at the front, incorporated entrances in a curve; the centre point of the auditorium, with its banked seats and gallery, was, as at Christ Church, the king's seat which was situated so that he, uniquely, had a clear view across the stage to the central arch.

Though the style of the Cockpit-in-Court was determined by antiquity, the performances for which it was built were not by the court amateurs, but by the professional players of which the King's Men were naturally pre-eminent. Their own venue Blackfriars, which Richard Burbage had re-opened in 1609, was inevitably something of a template for all indoor theatres.

John Webb (1611–72)

Educated at Merchant Taylor's School, Webb was possibly a kinsman of Inigo Jones whose office he joined in 1628. He was responsible for most of the surviving drawings of Jones's work (collected at Worcester College, Oxford) and author, or co-author with Jones, of *The Most Notable Antiquity of Great Britain vulgarly called Stone-Heng* (1655). He designed the scenery for *The Siege of Rhodes* at Davenant's Rutland House (1656).

Whitehall

The palace of Whitehall contained several spaces in which theatrical performances could be staged. The **Tudor Great Hall**, 12 by 26 m (39 by 87 feet), continued to be used for performances, of which the French pastoral *Florimene* in December 1635 by the Queen's Ladies with designs by Jones is particularly well documented.

It was to Jones that James I entrusted the design of the **Banqueting House**, the magnificent state hall which constituted the first truly Renaissance building of any size in England. Classical in design and constructed in stone – Oxfordshire, Northamptonshire and Portland – it stood in stark contrast to the timber and brick buildings which surrounded it. The building 34 m long, 17 m wide, 17 m high (111 feet long, 55 feet wide, 55 feet high) – a double cube, was still in the last stages of construction when Jonson's *The Masque of Augurs* was presented there on Twelfth Night 1622. The elaborate machinery required for this, and subsequent masques, was stored in the palace, the powerful lighting (torches) had a detrimental effect and performances were discontinued in 1635 principally out of concern for Rubens's great canvases newly installed on the ceiling. Sir William Davenant's *The Temple of Love* was the last masque to be performed in the Banqueting House.

The **Masquing House** was built as a replacement venue in 1637 at a cost of £2,500, a large amount for a wooden structure which was intended to be only temporary. It measured 37 m long, 17 m wide, 18 m high (120 feet long, 57 feet wide, 59 feet high) and, being designated for the performance of masques, was lavishly equipped with elaborate machinery. Though three spectacular masques (*Britannia Triumphans*, *Luminalia* and *Salmacida Spolia*) were performed there the times were not propitious for masques and monarchy. On 19 January 1642 King Charles I left his capital. He returned seven years later when the Banqueting House provided the backcloth for his execution.

Curtains

The outbreak of the Civil War in 1642 affected the theatres in advance of the execution of the king and the resulting Commonwealth. The long-standing – puritan – opposition now held sway within and beyond the city walls and one by one the theatres were razed to the ground.

Stowe's Annales

Play Houses. The Globe play house on the Bank side in Southwarke ... pulled downe to the ground, by Sir Matthew Brand, On Munday the 15 of April 1644, to make tenements in the room of it ... The Phenix [Cockpit] in Druery Lane, was pulled downe also [as was 'Salsbury Court'] this day, being Saterday the 24 day of March 1649, by the same solidiers ...

The Hope, on the Bank side in Southwarke commonly called the Beare Garden ... pulled down to make tenements, by Thomas Walker, a peticoate maker in Cannon Street, on Tuesday 25 March 1656.

The ravages of oppression and time both serve to show that theatre buildings are neither essential for performance nor enduring monuments to their art. Continuity between the Jacobean/Caroline stage and that of the Restoration was maintained by the survival of certain key individuals, of which the foremost was William Davenant, whose experience encompassed the Court masque and the public theatres. Ultimately it is the plays of a period which constitute its most durable legacy.

The playwrights

The masques to which Ben Jonson, George Chapman, Thomas Carew and Samuel Daniel devoted so much of their talent, though they survive in print, are never likely to be revived. They do, nevertheless, make interesting reading and provide invaluable information about their staging and the theatre of their day.

Thomas Middleton (c.1580–1627)

Middleton collaborated with **Thomas Dekker** (c.1572–1632) in *The Honest Whore* (1604) and *The Roaring Girl* (1610) and with **William Rowley** (c.1585–1626) in *The Changeling* (1622). His political satire *A Game of Chess* got him into trouble.

Sir Francis Beaumont (c.1584–1616) and John Fletcher (1579–1625)

Formed a famous partnership, though of up to 50 plays attributed to them only six or seven are authenticated.

John Webster (c.1580–1634)

Webster was the author of two enduring tragedies: *The White Devil* (1612) and *The Duchess of Malfi* (1614).

Philip Massinger (1583–1640)

Sir Giles Over-reach in Massinger's *A New Way to Pay Old Debts* (c.1625) has been a popular role for actors through the ages.

John Ford (1586–1640)

Of 'melancholy John Ford's' output his drama of incestuous love, *'Tis Pity She's a Whore* (c.1625–33) is regularly revived.

The impact of Serlio, Palladio and Aleotti was evident in the theatres constructed across Europe during the first half of the seventeenth century: the Hofburg in Vienna 1623, the Barbarini in Rome 1634, the Teatro Formigliari in Bologna 1640 and in Paris the Palais Cardinal, 1641, better known, following the death of Richelieu in 1642, as the Palais Royal.

5 [RE-]ENTER THE KING

On 29 May 1660, his birthday, King Charles II made a triumphant entry into London.

John Evelyn (1620–1706) *Diary*

With a triumph of above 20,000 horse and foote, brandishing their swords, and shouting with inexpressible joy; the wayes strew'd with flowers, the bells ringing, the streetes hung with tapissry, fountaines, running with wine, the Maior, Aldermen, and all the Companies in their liveries, chaines of gold, and banners; Lords and Nobles ... trumpets and music, and myriads of people flocking ...

That his subjects should celebrate their sovereign's return with such exuberant pageantry reflected the deprivation from which they had suffered during his absence and expressed their need for colour and excitement, which – in the form of theatre – had been denied them for 18 years.

With nearly half a million inhabitants London was home to 7 per cent of the nation's population and 15 times more populous than the next largest cities, Bristol and Norwich. Paris, though the largest city in Europe, contained only 2.5 per cent of the population of France.

The king in exile

Such comparisons would not have been lost on Charles II who had gone into exile in 1646, three years before his father's execution, returning only briefly and ingloriously, following his proclamation as King of Scotland, to face defeat at the Battle of Worcester in September 1651. Charles had spent the early years of his exile in France, but after 1654 he travelled in Germany and the Spanish Netherlands. During these years the future king experienced acute poverty, which in part accounted for his subsequent extravagance but, in the words of his future poet laureate **John Dryden**

(1631–1700), he had 'an opportunity which is rarely allowed to sovereign princes ... of travelling and being conversant in the most polished courts of Europe'.

Of these courts that of Louis XIV (1638–1715) was in the early and troubled stages of its progress to pre-eminence in Europe, but the young king had already developed a passion for the arts, the theatre in particular, which he pursued enthusiastically despite opposition in some influential quarters.

Paris theatres

Paris had never had open-air theatres like those in London. The city's longest-established theatre was the Théâtre de l'Hotel de Bourgogne, which dated back to 1548 when the *hotel* (town mansion) of the Dukes of Burgundy was partly demolished and a theatre built on the site. The Hotel de Bourgogne was a long, narrow room with a platform stage (using a traditional simultaneous setting) at one end with a pit for standing spectators extending to tiers of benches with boxes along the sides. It is the setting for Act 1 of Edmond Rostand's *Cyrano de Bergerac* (1897) which takes place in 1640.

Les acteurs

In the cast of Rostand's play is **Zacharie Jacob Montfleury** (c.1600–67) an enormously fat man with a loud voice and pompous delivery, he is depicted as a figure of fun by Rostand.

Pierre Le Messier Bellerose (c.1600–70) was acclaimed for both comedy and tragedy. Though rhetorical, his style was quieter and he helped to raise the status of the legitimate (rather than farcical) actor.

Julian Bedeau Jodelet (c.1600–60) was a white-faced comedian whose appearance raised an immediate laugh. He would make his own additions to the author's dialogue.

In France from the outset the professional theatre engaged actresses.

Until 1634 the Confraternity of the Passion, which controlled the Hôtel de Bourgogne, enjoyed a monopoly, but that year Cardinal Richelieu encouraged a rival company under the distinguished actor **Guillaume Montdory** (1594–1651) to set up at the Marais Theatre, formerly a tennis court. A healthy rivalry was thereby created between Richelieu's Montdory company at the Marais and the King's Players (Comediens du Roi) at the Bourgogne. The Marais was rebuilt – following a fire – in 1644, as was the Bourgogne in 1647, so that with the Palais Cardinal (1641)/Palais Royal (1642) Paris had three modern theatres. Others followed, culminating in the Comédie-Française, designed by François d'Orbay, which opened on 18 April 1689.

Corneille and Racine

In his early career Pierre Corneille (1606–84) spanned comedy, tragedy and tragi-comedy (*Clitandre* 1631). One of five authors commissioned to write plays for him by Richelieu, Corneille offended his patron by changing the plot which had been allocated to him. He deserted Paris for Rouen where he wrote his masterpiece *Le Cid*, which was performed at the Marais in 1636/7 with Montdory as the hero Rodrigue and **Marguerite de Villiers** (?–1670) as Chimene. Corneille strained the classical unities of time, place and action to relate the events of what has been described as the most crowded day in all recorded time.

Spain

For his drama of Spain's national hero Corneille drew upon the pair of chronicle plays, *Las Mocedades del Cid* by **Castro y Bellvis** (1569–1631). The Spanish theatre, with its open-air playhouses resembling those in London, had been tremendously energetic and productive. **Lope de Vega's** (1562–1635) position as the world's most prolific playwright is unlikely to be seriously challenged, even though his own claim to have written 1,500 plays has been reduced to around 314 by modern scholarship. **Pedro Calderon de la Barga** (1600–81), who wrote his first play at 14, is credited with about 200 works ranging from comedy to history and religious.

Corneille's *Le Cid* was soon seen and admired in Spain and an English version by Joseph Rutter was performed in London by Beeston's Boys in 1637. The international 'hit' play is not a recent phenomenon.

Jean Racine (1639–99) entered into direct competition with Corneille in 1670, when they both produced plays on the same subject (Racine's *Bérénice*, Corneille's *Tite et Bérénice*). Racine's masterpiece, *Phèdre*, followed in 1677 but, though widely admired, it also fuelled the jealousy of lesser rivals with the result that Racine abandoned the professional stage. His two biblical plays *Esther* (1689) and *Athalie* (1690) were performed privately by the young ladies of Saint-Cyr at the request of Madame de Maintenan. Racine's first play – *La Thébaide* – had been staged at the Palais Royal by Molière who, by then – 1664–, had established himself not only as an inspired comic actor but as a dramatist of genius.

Lt vray Portrait de Mr de Molière en Habit de Sganarelle.

Molière in the character of Sganarelle

Molière (1622–73)

On 27 April 1621 Jean Poquelin, a well-to-do marchant-tapissier (royal upholsterer) married the daughter of Louis Cressé, also a marchant-tapissier; on 15 January 1622 – 'promptly, but decently' – their son Jean-Baptiste, whom the world would know as Molière, was born. The boy received a good education at the Jesuit College of Clermont, an establishment favoured by the aristocracy, where he engaged in performances of plays by Plautus, Terence and Seneca. After studying and qualifying (1642) in law, Jean-Baptiste was poised to succed his father as marchant-tapissier but, instead, changed his name to Molière and embarked on a stage career.

Molière's first enterprise, L'Illustre Théâtre, in which his mistress **Madeleine Béjart** (1618–72) was his professional partner, was short-lived (1643–5) but he persevered and – after a brief spell in prison – joined a touring company of players. Molière gradually took over the running of the troupe, gained a reputation as an actor, had his first two plays staged and, on 24 October 1658, performed at the Louvre before Louis XIV. The king authorized the company's establishment at the Théâtre du Petit-Bourbon in Paris with his brother, the Duke of Anjou as their patron, thereby acquiring the title of 'La Troupe de Monsieur'.

Though no stranger to controversy – both *The School for Wives* (1663) and *Tartuffe* (1664) provoked strong opposition, the latter for its depiction of religion – Molière continued to enjoy the patronage and protection of Louis XIV, whose confidence was rewarded by *The Misanthrope* (1666), *The Miser* (1668) and *The Hypochondriac* (1673).

Molière's personal life was less successful. His marriage in 1662 to **Amande Béjart** (1642–1700) was deeply unhappy, though by way of compensation to posterity, if not themselves, it provided the raw material for *The Misanthrope* in which the ill-suited couple appeared as Alceste and Célimène. Amande, ostensibly the sister of Molière's former mistress Madeleine Béjart, was said by some to be her daughter and by others – the rival actor Montfleury – to be Molière's too.

Molière's own ill-health brought authenticity to his four performances as Argan in *The Hypochondriac* after the fourth of which, on 17 February 1673, he died. Even in death, Molière needed his royal patron, through whose intervention he was buried in holy ground which the church authorities had initially refused.

Molière succeeded in elevating the status of comedy to a parity with tragedy. He drew upon Plautus and Terence, *commedia dell'arte*, *comedie-ballet* (akin to the English Court masque); he absorbed farce within the literary – usually verse – form of the five-act play and he imbued it with psychological insight and social comment.

Some English imitators

Of the many English dramatists who were more or less indebted to Molière the following stand as examples:

John Dryden *Sir Martin Marr-all* (1667), based on *L'Étourdi*; **William Wycherley** *The Plain Dealer* (1667), based on *Le Misanthrope*; **John Vanbrugh** *The Mistake* (1704) based on *Le Dépit Amoureux*.

Raising the curtain

Even before the official re-opening of the theatres by Charles II there were a few exceptions to the ban on performance. Of these, by far the most significant was *The Siege of Rhodes*.

Davenant's address to the Reader in *The Siege of Rhodes*, September 1656

Sire William Davenant: *The Siege of Rhodes*. Made a representation by the art of prospective in scenes and the story sung in recitative music. At the back of Rutland House in the upper end of Aldersgate Street, London.

John Webb had to accommodate the scenery on a stage 7 m (22 feet) wide, 5 m (15 feet) deep and 3 m (11 feet) high. The designs, at Chatsworth House in Derbyshire, reveal his solution. He provided

1. a 'frontis piece', in effect a proscenium arch
2. a number of pairs of border-wings, at each side of the stage, parallel with the front
3. a number of hanging borders across the stage linking with the side wings (2)
4. shutters, made up of a pair of flats, one from each side of the stage, meeting in the middle to form a complete picture

5 at the back of the stage the 'relieve'/relief scene, made up of cut-out planes against a backcloth, giving the sense of three dimensions.

The 'relieve' scenes (Solyman's Throne; Mount Philermus) were prepared behind the shutters and revealed when these were drawn apart.

Of Webb's designs for *The Siege of Rhodes* Jocelyn Powell has written:

The combination of the painted scenery with its wings and shutters giving the illusion of depth, and the relieve scene giving further depth behind, became basic to the scenic design of the Restoration, and the interaction of deep with comparatively shallow scenic effects gave the plays much of their rhythmic impulse.

(*Restoration Theatre Production*, p.41)

Thus one of the most significant features of the Restoration stage preceded the king's return, but that is not to diminish the scale of his contribution to the theatre of his reign and beyond.

King Charles as patron

Following the example of Louis XIV, Charles II was determined to be an active patron of the drama and the theatre. **Sir Samuel Tukes** (?–1674), a courtier who had shared the king's exile, listed Charles' accomplishments: three languages (Spanish, Italian, French), knowledge of ancient and modern history, an understanding of mathematics and a delight in navigation, before concluding 'in General, here is a true friend to Literature, and to Learned Men'.

At the king's suggestion Tukes wrote a play, *The Adventures of Five Hours*, a tragicomedy adapted from the Spanish dramatist Calderon, which was highly praised by **Samuel Pepys** (1633–1703). Charles also encouraged other aristocrats in their playwriting aspirations: the **Earl of Bristol**, the **Earl of Orrery** (1621–79), **Tom D'Urfey** (1653–1723), **John Crowne** (?–1640–1703 or 1714) and **John Dryden**.

Playwrights need actors and at the very outset of his reign King Charles II took the necessary measures to ensure that provision.

The patents

On 21 August 1660 the king granted theatrical patents to **Thomas Killigrew**, whose company – the King's Company – enjoyed the monarch's own patronage and to **William Davenant**, whose company known as the Duke's Company had the king's brother, the Duke of York, as its patron. Both men had been close associates of the king during his exile and had worked in the theatre prior to the closure in 1642.

Warrant granted by Charles II to Killigrew and Davenant, 21 August 1660

Charles the Second, by the grace of God, of England, Scotland and Ireland, King, Defender of the Faith, etc – Whereas we are given to understand that certain persons in and about our City of London, or the suburbs thereof, do frequently assemble for the performing and acting of plays and interludes for rewards, to which diverse of our subjects do for their entertainment resort; which said plays, as we are informed, do contain much matter of profanation and scurrility, so that such kind of entertainments which if well managed might serve as moral instructions in human life ... We, taking the premises into our princely consideration, yet not holding it necessary totally to suppress the use of theatres ... do hereby give and grant unto the said Thomas Killigrew and Sir William Davenant full power and authority to erect two companies of players ... and to purchase, build and erect or hire at their charge ... two houses or theatres ... for the representation of tragedies, comedies, plays, operas and all other entertainments of this nature in convenient places ...

Thomas Killigrew (1612–83)

Killigrew began his theatrical career as a child, appearing as a devil at the Red Bull Theatre. He had written several plays before the closure of the theatres in 1642; all were tragi-comedies of which *The Parson's Wedding*, based on Calderon and first performed in 1640, was revived in 1664 with an all-female cast causing even Pepys to blush. During the inter-regnum Killigrew shared his king's exile, travelling extensively around Europe. His experiences provided material for his semi-autobiographical play *Thomas the Wanderer* (c.1654).

Sir William Davenant (1608–68)

Born and educated in Oxford, Davenant was reputed to be the natural son of William Shakespeare and the hostess of the Crown Inn, Cornmarket. Though Shakespeare was Davenant's godfather there is no proof of his paternity.

Davenant's first play *The Cruel Brother* was performed in 1627 and in 1640 he was responsible for the last Court masque *Salmacida Spolia*. He succeeded Ben Jonson as poet laureate in 1638 and Beeston as manager of the Cockpit Theatre, Drury Lane in 1640. Knighted by Charles I in 1643, Davenant, who undertook various missions for the king, was captured and imprisoned in the Tower of London (1650–2). He subsequently joined Charles in Paris, but returned home and succeeded in staging *The Siege of Rhodes*, generally regarded as the first English opera.

Finance

Davenant and Killigrew had petitioned Charles II for their patents. The patents brought certain privileges. Some of the actors were liveried as Grooms of the Chamber; they could appeal to the king if in difficulty and they enjoyed immunity from arrest except on the Lord Chamberlain's warrant. The companies received no financial retainer, just fees of £20 for performing at Court and £10 when the king attended their theatre. Furthermore the companies had to have their plays licensed by the Revels Office at the rate of £2 for a new play, £1 for a revival. Prestigious though the patents were the holders (supposedly in perpetuity) occupied no sinecure. As Jocelyn Powell has observed: 'Like the society in which it lived, the Restoration theatre was Janus-faced, looking one way towards the glamorous patronage of the Court and another toward its own independent development as a commercial institution.' (*Restoration Theatre Production*, p.147) The two managers adopted different commercial practices. Davenant's company was essentially a co-operative in which the members shared the proceeds of each performance after the direct costs had been deducted. Killigrew paid a set £3.10s (£3.50) per acting day to everyone who had put capital into his venture. Of the two methods Davenant's proved to be the more successful.

The theatre

Clearly the major outlay for the patentees was a building in which to perform. Of the pre-1642 theatres the Red Bull, which Killigrew briefly occupied and Pepys attended on 23 May 1661 to find 'not one hundred in the whole house', and the Cockpit in Drury Lane had survived, but no longer matched the needs of performers or playgoers.

Instead, Killigrew and Davenant – like many theatre managers before and after them – made use of the most suitable existing buildings they could find: tennis courts in London.

Killigrew set up at Gibbon's Tennis Court in Vere Street, off Clare Market in November 1660. Davenant opened Lisle's Tennis Court in Portugal Street, Lincoln's Inn Fields in June 1661 with a revival of an expanded version of *The Siege of Rhodes*. As at Rutland House the production was promoted for its use of perspective scenery. In contrast Killigrew eschewed scenery, recreating the style of staging used at earlier (indoor and outdoor) English public theatres. Evidently the public was not content and, in 1663, Killigrew moved to a former riding school in Bridges Street off Drury Lane where he could mount more elaborate staging. Not to be outdone Davenant commissioned Sir Christopher Wren to design a theatre in Dorset Garden, near to the Thames, just south of Fleet Street. The Duke's Theatre, as it was known, having cost £9,000, opened with a capacity of 1,000–1,200 in 1671, but by then Davenant was dead.

In 1672 Killigrew's Bridge Street Theatre was burnt down and he also turned to Wren, who designed what was to be the first Drury Lane Theatre which opened in 1674.

Sir Christopher Wren (1632–1723)

Best known as the architect of St Paul's Cathedral, Wren was also responsible for 52 churches in London – following the Great Fire of 1666 – and the Sheldonian Theatre in Oxford. Amongst Wren's drawings in All Souls College, Oxford is a longitudinal scale section of a building labelled 'Playhouse'. The length of this building corresponds closely to that of the site, about 34 m by 18 m (112 feet by 59 feet), in Drury Lane and, although there is no conclusive proof that his design represents the building as constructed, it provides evidence of Wren's concept. The auditorium consists of a sloping pit, two tiers of boxes and an upper gallery; the stage, though framed by a proscenium arch, incorporated a platform thrusting into the auditorium with two stage doors on either side, and a scenic area with grooves and shutters extending to a vista at the rear. Wren's design has been described as 'a marriage between the Italian scenic stage and the English platform stage' (Donald C. Mullin *The Development of the English Playhouse*, p.67) in which 'the actors had the benefit of a suggestion of place, and the freedom of an uncluttered acting platform; and they could also be discovered within the scene, and surrounded by such scenic illusion as was necessary'.

Wren's design established the model for English theatre architecture until well into the next century. His Drury Lane, substantially altered by the Adam brothers in 1775, lasted until 1791. Its foundations remain beneath the present theatre.

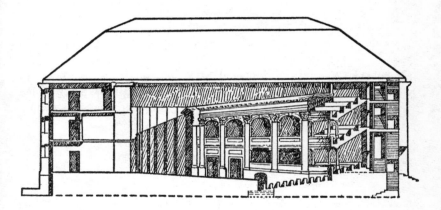

Christopher Wren's theatre design, probably for Drury Lane, 1674

Audiences

The capacity of Wren's theatre has been put as high as 2,000. The economics of Drury Lane and other theatres of the period have been the subject of much speculation. Entry to the upper gallery was 1s (5p), the equivalent of two chickens, the middle gallery 1s 6d (7.5p) and for the best seats in the lower gallery boxes and pit 2s 6d (12.5p). On 6 January 1668 Samuel Pepys paid 20s (£1) for a whole box for himself and his companions. At that time his cook-maid was paid £4 a year. Clearly the auditorium was very hierarchical with the quick-witted courtiers close to the actors and the duller citizens further back. Orange sellers plied their wares, as did members of 'the oldest profession'. Individuals in the audience often attracted more attention than the action on the stage.

John Crowne epilogue to *Sir Courtly Nice*, 1685

Our Galleries too, were finely us'd of late,
Where roosting Masques sat cackling for a Mate;
They came not to see Plays but act their own,
And had throng'd Audiences when we had none.
Our Plays it was impossible to hear,
The honest Country Men were forc't to swear:
Confound you, give your bawdy prating o're.
Or Zounds, I'le fling you i' the Pit, you bawling Whore.

Nevertheless it must be remembered that the plays of the period abound in wit, double meanings and intellectual skirmishing, and it says much for the skill of the performers and the mettle of the audiences that an authentic theatrical engagement took place in such circumstances.

Actors

The cost of performance has been calculated at £25–35. Actors' salaries ranged from 10s (50p) for apprentices to 50s (£2.50) for leading actresses, £4 for senior actors, £5 for Thomas Betterton (see overleaf). Actors who were also share-holders under the Davenant system received a proportion of any profit. But the theatre was not very profitable and such was the financial crisis for both companies in 1681 that they merged.

As in the Elizabethan/Jacobean theatre the actors received 'parts' with cue-lines. Rehearsals, supervised by the prompter, were devoted to working out entrances and exits, with the individual actors being left to their own devices as far as their movement about the stage was concerned. The action tended to be concentrated on the fore-stage where the lighting was better and the audience's attention could be more easily engaged.

Killigrew's company

Killigrew drew on the corps of veterans who had mustered at the old Red Bull Theatre. Foremost amongst these was **Michael Mohun** (c.1620–84), a boy-actor under Beeston, who was playing adult roles before the closure of the theatres. During the Civil War he had been a major in the Royalist forces. He was accomplished in both tragedy and comedy. **Charles Hart** (c.1620–84) had also been a boy-actor and then a Royalist soldier. Heroic parts were his forte; Alexander in *The Rival Queens* (Nathaniel Lee – 1677) being a particular success. **Edward Kynaston** (c.1640–1706) was the last 'boy-player' specializing in female roles. Pepys said that 'he made the loveliest lady that I ever saw' and Colley Cibber recounted that King Charles had to wait for the start of the play whilst Kynaston, who played the tragedy queen, was being shaved. Killigrew established a training school for actors.

Davenant's company

Davenant assembled a company comprised mainly of the younger generation of actors. Of these Thomas Betterton proved to be pre-eminent.

Thomas Jevon (?–1688) was a celebrated Harlequin, who also wrote plays.

James Nokes (?–1696) could reduce audiences to laughter by his looks alone. He was renowned for his performances of gullible old husbands and foppish suitors.

Samuel Sandford (fl. 1660–99) was a master of facial expression who specialized in more-or-less villainous characters earning himself the description 'the best Villain in the World' from Charles II.

Thomas Betterton (1635–1710)

When John Rhodes, the bookseller to whom he was apprenticed, re-opened the Cockpit in Drury Lane, Betterton's talent as an actor was immediately evident and he was soon established as the star of Davenant's company.

His Shakespearean roles (albeit often in adaptations) included Mercutio, Hamlet, King Lear, Macbeth and Henry VIII. As Hamlet he was coached by Davenant who had seen Joseph Taylor, who had been 'instructed by the author' in the role. A famous Bosola in *The Duchess of Malfi*, for Congreve

Betterton created Heartwell in *The Old Bachelor* (1693), Maskwell in *The Double Dealer* (1694), Valentine in *Love for Love* (1695) and Fainall in *The Way of the World* (1700).

Betterton was also a share-holder in the Duke's Company and, after Davenant's death, its co-manager, leading it into its new Dorset Garden Theatre, staying there until the merger of the companies in 1682. In 1695 Betterton re-opened the Lincoln's Inn Fields Theatre staying there until 1705 when the company moved to Vanbrugh's new Queen's Theatre in the Haymarket.

Betterton twice travelled to France to see the new spectacular scenery in use there and he also wrote and adapted plays, but it was as an actor (over 120 roles can be credited to him) that he gained true eminence. His acting was free from rant and exaggeration.

His Actions were few, but just ...
his Aspect was serious, venerable and majestic ...
His Voice was low and grumbling, yet he could Time it
by an artful *Climax* which enforc'd universal Attention,
even from the *Fops* and *Orange-girls* ...

Anthony Aston, *A Brief Supplement to Colley Cibber* ... 1748

he made the Ghost (in *Hamlet*) equally terrible to the Spectator, as to himself ...

Colley Cibber, *An Apology for the life of Colley Cibber*, 1740

Enter the actress

In 1662 Betterton married **Mary Sanderson** (?–1712), one of the first English actresses, whom Pepys always identified with Ianthe in Davenant's *The Siege of Rhodes*. She was also a notable Lady Macbeth. Her husband was often partnered by **Mrs Elizabeth Barry** (1658–1713). The title Mrs was honorific as Elizabeth Barry never married and was recurrently associated with scandal in her private life. On stage she exuded power and dignity in roles such as Belvidera in Otway's *Venice Preserved* (1681).

Mrs Barry

Mrs Barry, in Characters of Greatness, had a Presence of elevated
dignity, her Mien and Motion superb, and gracefully majestick, her
voice full, clear, and strong, so that no Violence of Passion could be
too much for her.

Cibber

In contrast, **Mrs Anne Bracegirdle** (c.1663–1748) excelled in genteel
comedy and strenuously upheld the probity of her private life.

Mrs Bracegirdle

As when she acted Millament (in Congreve's *The Way of the World*)
all the Faults, Follies and Affectation of that agreeable Tyrant were
venially melted down into so many Charms, and Attractions of a
conscious Beauty.

Cibber

Mrs Bracegirdle's successor was **Anne (Nance) Oldfield** (1683–1730)
who was endowed with a beautiful face and figure and a wonderfully
distinctive voice. Although she has successes in tragedy (Rowe's *Jane
Shore* 1714) she preferred and indeed excelled in comedy especially as
Sylvia in Farquhar's *The Recruiting Officer* (1706) and Mrs Sullen in *The
Beaux Stratagem* (1707).

Breeches parts

This was the convention that young romantic male roles should be played
by women. Sir Harry Wildair in Farquhar's *The Constant Couple* belonged
in Peg Wolfington's performance to this tradition, as do the principal boys
in pantomime.

Restoration audiences also relished the display of parts of the female
anatomy which were revealed when characters such as Margery Pinchwife
in Wycherley's *The Country Wife* (1675) and Sylvia in Farquhar's *The
Recruiting Officer* adopt male disguise.

Shakespeare

Actresses performing the many heroines who assume male identity added to the enduring attractions of Shakespeare's comedies, but many of his plays were no longer deemed to be acceptable unless they were adapted to contemporary taste.

Thus *The Taming of the Shrew* became John Lacy's *Sawny the Scot* (1667); Dryden and Davenant revised *The Tempest* (also 1667), but the most durable adaptation was *The History of King Lear* (1681) by **Nahum Tate** (1652–1715), later poet laureate 1693, now completed with a happy ending.

EDGAR: Our drooping Country now erects her Head,
           Peace spreads her balmy Wings; and Plenty Blooms.
           Divine *Cordelia*, all the Gods can witness
           How much thy Love to Empire I prefer!
           Thy bright example shall convince the World
           (Whatever Storms of Fortune are decreed)
           That Truth and Vertue shall at last succeed.

                    [*Exeunt Omnes*]

The plays

Charles II's high-flown aspiration, expressed in his 1660 warrant to the patentees, that plays 'might serve as moral instructions in human life', had not been borne out. Indeed the theatre had become increasingly associated with immorality and vice. The dramatists were not defenceless for, as Kenneth Muir has written: 'it is arguable that a dramatist who wishes to satirise the sexual behaviour of his age is bound to be indecent. The more moral he is, the more indecent he will be.' (*The Comedy of Manners*, p.20)

On the other hand the more overt and outrageous the depiction of sexuality becomes the greater the risk that spectators, far from being discouraged, will be drawn into similar indulgence. Restoration playgoers certainly had ample opportunities to put these arguments to the test. With runs of new plays still averaging only three or four nights – *The Old Bachelor* broke records with 14 consecutive performances in 1693 – the demand for new plays was still considerable with about 440 being produced between 1660 and 1700.

The dramatists

Sir George Etherege (c.1636–92) author of *She Would If She Could* (1668) and *The Man of Mode* (1676). The latter play includes the quintessential fop, Sir Fopling Flutter, and the heartless witty libertine Dorimant, thought by many to be a portrait of **Lord Rochester** (1647–80) whose many mistresses included Elizabeth Barry.

John Dryden (1631–1700), poet (laureate), critic, satirist and author of nearly 30 plays of all kinds, of which *All For Love*, his version of the Antony and Cleopatra story, is regarded as his masterpiece.

William Wycherley (1640–1716), much indebted to Molière, though of a coarser strain, his most enduring play is *The Country Wife* (1674–5).

Mrs Aphra Behn (1640–89), the author of at least 17 plays, was the first professional English woman playwright. She used some of her personal exploits as material for her dramas which are as robust and outspoken as those of her male contemporaries. *The Rover* (1677) and *The Lucky Chance* (1686) still hold the stage.

Thomas Otway (1652–85), the author of *Venice Preserved*; or, *Plot Discovered* (1682) which was highly topical at the time of Monmouth's rebellion.

William Congreve (1670–1729), the supreme stylist of the Restoration stage, his plays were closely associated with Betterton's performances. *The Way of the World* (1700), his consummate achievement, endures as a lasting adornment of the English-speaking stage.

Colley Cibber (1671–1757) actor, playwright, manager and author of *Apology for The Life of Mr Colley Cibber, Comedian* (1740). In his plays he sought to strike a balance between satirical and sentimental comedy. As an actor he was celebrated as Lord Foppington in Vanbrugh's *The Relapse*.

Sir John Vanbrugh (1664–1726) was the only dramatist to have designed a theatre – the Queen's in the Haymarket which suffered from appalling acoustics. He was more successful as the architect of Blenheim Palace and Castle Howard and the author of *The Relapse* (1696).

George Farquhar 1678–1707 was the last of the Restoration dramatists, but in his short life he produced three lasting plays: *The Constant Couple* (1699), *The Recruiting Officer* (1706) and *The Beaux Stratagem* (1707).

Jeremy Collier (1650–1726)

A political pamphleteer and a non-juring clergyman who refused to swear the oath of allegiance to William and Mary. He voiced the mounting criticism of the – alleged – immorality of the stage. To Collier the stage was corrupting society rather than reflecting a society that was already corrupt. Nevertheless Collier did not wish to suppress the theatre, but to improve it.

A Short View of the Immorality and Profaneness of the English Stage, 1697–98

The Business of Plays is to recommend Vertue, and discountenance Vice; to shew the Uncertainty of Humane Greatness, the suddain Turns of Fate and the unhappy Conclusions of Violence and Injustice. 'Tis to expose the Singularities of Pride and Fancy, to make Folly and Falsehood contemptible and to bring every Thing that is ill under Infamy and Neglect …

These advantages are now in the Enemies Hand, and under a very dangerous Management. Like Cannon seized, they are pointed the wrong way …

In retrospect the Restoration stage seems to some to be remote and hopelessly anachronistic, but it established the shape of the English playhouse for generations to come and produced a remarkable body of lasting plays which, for all their apparent artifice, get to the heart of human nature.

6 | THE DRAMA'S LAWS

Dr Johnson's famous couplet 'The drama's laws the drama's patrons give, / For we that live to please must please to live' was amply borne out in the eighteenth century during which the theatre had to balance the demands of authority with those of an increasingly democratic clientele.

The Beggar's Opera

Charles Macklin (c.1699–1797), the Irish actor and dramatist, recorded his visit to **John Gay**'s (1685–1732) ballad opera *The Beggar's Opera* at Lincoln's Inn Fields in 1728.

> In the scene where Peacham and Lockit are described settling their accounts (II.X.Air xxx) Lockit sings the song
>
> When you censure the age etc
>
> Which had such an effect on the audience that, as if by instinct, the greater part of them threw their eyes on the stage box where the Minister [Sir Robert Walpole, Prime Minister] was sitting and loudly *encored* it; for no sooner was the song finished then he *encored* it a second time himself, joined in the general applause, and by this means brought the audience into so much good humour with him that they gave him a general huzza from all parts of the house.
>
> William Cooke, *Memoirs of Charles Macklin*, 1804, p.53

Gay's comparison of contemporary politicians, Walpole in particular, with highwaymen and their criminal associates was immensely popular 'making Gay rich and Rich gay', but Walpole, for all his sangfroid at the performance attended by Macklin, thereafter 'never could with any satisfaction be present at its representation on account of the many allusions which the audience thought referred to his character'. The theatre had shown its capacity to sting politicians, but they in their turn sought means to prevent such attacks.

John Rich (c.1682–1761)

John Rich was the son of **Christopher Rich** (?–1714) a devious lawyer who acquired the Drury Lane patent but so alienated the company that he was forced out to Lincoln's Inn Fields. There, from 1716, John Rich produced a series of highly successful pantomimes with himself, under the stage name of John Lun, as Harlequin.

> To retrieve the credit of this theatre, Rich created a species of dramatic composition unknown to this, and, I believe, to any other country, which he called pantomime ... he interwove a comic fable, consisting chiefly of the courtship of Harlequin and Columbine with a variety of surprising adventures and tricks, which were produced by the magic wand of Harlequin; such as the sudden transformation of palaces and temples to huts and cottages; of men and women into wheel-barrows ...
>
> from Thomas Dance's *Memoirs of the Life of David Garrick*,
> 1808, p.130

John Rich flourished to the extent that he could raise £6,000 by subscription to build a new theatre, Covent Garden Theatre, which opened on 7 December 1732 with a revival of Congreve's *The Way of the World*. Closely modelled on Wren's Drury Lane, Convent Garden had a larger capacity achieved by a reduction in the size of the fore-stage and the extension of the galleries (the second gallery had 16 rows of benches compared with four at Drury Lane).

Censorship

Throughout history, authority (the Church, monarchs, governments) has tried to control the theatre. The success of *The Beggar's Opera* prompted a vogue for political satire of which **Henry Fielding** (1705–54) was a noted exponent. The venues for these plays were not the patent houses, but the smaller, unlicensed Lincoln's Inn Fields, Goodman's Fields (1729, rebuilt in 1733) and the Little Theatre in the Haymarket (1720). Concern was shared by the politicians, who were the butts of the satire, the Lord Mayor and Aldermen of the City of London, the patent managers and their financial backers. Things reached a head in March 1737 when Walpole was alerted to the forthcoming production of the scurrilous *The Vision of the Golden Rump* at Goodman's Fields. He acted swiftly. The Bill presented to the House of Commons on 20 May received the Royal Assent on 21 June 1737.

The Licensing Act restricted the monarch's power to grant theatrical patents in the City of Westminster only during his residence, thereby effectively closing down the small theatres and leaving Drury Lane and Covent Garden secure in their monopoly (Vanbrugh's theatre had virtually become the preserve of opera). The Act also strengthened regulations about vagrancy in the provinces, but its most enduring stipulation was that concerning the licensing of plays by the Lord Chamberlain which remained in force until 1968. Theatre managers were required to submit a copy of 'any new interlude, tragedy, comedy, opera, play, farce or other entertainment of the stage ... to the Lord Chamberlain of the King's household ... fourteen days at least before the acting, representing or performing thereof.' The same rule applied to 'any new act, scene or part' added to an existing piece and to 'any new prologue or epilogue'. The penalty was £50 and the forfeit of the licence.

David Garrick (1717–79)

David Garrick, who as an actor, manager and playwright was to dominate the mid-eighteenth century English theatre, was bent not upon challenging but on enlisting the support of all in positions of prestige and authority. Born in Hereford, Garrick grew up in Lichfield where he attended **Dr Johnson**'s (1709–84) school. In 1737 pupil and master moved to London where the former pursued a career in the wine trade, but on 19 October 1741 Garrick made his professional acting debut at Goodman's Fields as Richard III. The manager **Henry Giffard** (1694–1772) evaded the law by charging admission, 1s, 2s, 3s (5p, 10p, 15p), for a concert in the middle of which a play was performed at no extra charge.

Actor

Garrick's natural style of acting was an immediate revelation for audiences accustomed to **James Quin** (1693–1766) whose declamatory, unvarying delivery was accompanied by equally unyielding, laboured gestures. The distinctive quality of Garrick's acting is captured by Henry Fielding in *Tom Jones* (1749).

Mr Partridge at *Hamlet* on which of the Players he had liked best

'The King without Doubt.' 'Indeed, Mr Partridge,' says Mrs Miller, 'you are not of the same opinion as the Town, for they are all agreed that Hamlet is acted by the best Player who ever was on the Stage.' 'He the best Player!' cries Partridge, with a contemptuous Sneer, 'Why, I could act as well as he myself. I am sure if I had seen a Ghost, I should have looked in the same Manner and done just as he did ... I know you are only joking with me; but indeed, Madam, though I was never at a Play in *London*, yet I have seen acting before in the Country; and the King for my money; he speaks all his Words distinctly, half as loud again as the other – Any Body may see he is an Actor.

As an actor Garrick was acclaimed in tragedy (Romeo, Hamlet, Macbeth, King Lear) and comedy (Benedick, Abel Drugger in *The Alchemist* and Sir John Brute in Vanbrugh's *The Provok'd Wife*.) The following description of Garrick as Drugger expresses the actor's subtlety.

David Garrick as King Lear

Garrick as Abel Drugger

When the astrologers spell out from the stars the name Abel Drugger, henceforth to be great, the poor gullible creature says with heartfelt delight: 'That is my name' … to himself. The effect of this judicious restraint is indescribable, for one did not see him merely as a simpleton being gulled, but as a much more ridiculous creature, with an air of secret triumph, thinking himself the slyest of rogues.

Georg Christoph Lichtenberg

Manager

Garrick could have made and kept his reputation as an actor alone but, for 29 years from April 1747, he was actively engaged in the management of Drury Lane Theatre. During that time he engaged actors of varying talents. The aforementioned Quin made intermittent performances as did **Spranger Barry** (1719–77) with whom Garrick enjoyed partnership – as Jaffier and Pierre in *Venice Preserved* – and, more often, a rivalry, especially when Barry was Covent Garden's counter-attraction. Charles Macklin, who had coached Garrick and for a time shared a *ménage à trois* with him and the actress Peg Woffington, opened Garrick's management with his innovative Shylock. Regular supporting actors included comedians **Harry Woodward** (1717–77) and **Richard Yates** (1706–96) and the character actor **Tom King** (1730–1804) who created Sir Peter Teazle in Sheridan's *The School for Scandal* (1777).

Garrick acted with leading ladies of differing styles. **Susanna Cibber** (1714–66) the second wife of Theophilus Cibber (Colley's son) and Dr Arne's sister who, having been trained as a singer, retained a high-pitched, recitative style of delivery in her stage roles such as Juliet. In contrast, **Mrs (Hannah) Pritchard** (1711–68), though formed in the school of Quin, showed more nature and variety. Both Johan Zoffany and Henry Fuseli captured – in their different ways – Garrick and Mrs Pritchard as Macbeth and Lady Macbeth. Beautiful and vivacious, **Peg Woffington** (c.1714–60) excelled as high-spirited ladies of quality, such as Millament in *The Way of the World* and in breeches parts, being incomparable as Sir Harry Wildair in *The Constant Couple*. Her relationship with other actresses was often tempestuous – especially so with **George Anne Bellamy** (c.1727–88) and **Kitty Clive** (1711–85).

Although Garrick was a fine judge of female talent on stage (and not immune to its charms off) following his marriage in 1749 to Eva Marie Violetti, a dancer, he became a model of respectability. In 1754 he purchased a riverside estate with gardens by Capability Brown at Hampton, though his neighbour Horace Walpole perceived his apparent refinement as evidence of his mimic ability rather than genuine gentility.

As a manager Garrick had to contend with ungentlemanly behaviour by his patrons. Following the enlargement of the Drury Lane auditorium in 1762 Garrick introduced two reforms. The exclusion of spectators from the stage, which had been effected at the Comédie Français in 1759, was successful, but the abolition of the half-priced system for admission after the third act was greeted with such violent opposition that Garrick had to retract.

France

In disgust Garrick abandoned the stage and spent the next two years on the continent where, especially in France, he was feted by actors, writers and intellectuals. The Parisian theatres of the day were engaged in various innovations.

Count Francesco Algarotti (1712–64) had been advocating greater illusion in scenery, costume, lighting and acting, upholding the example of **Ferdinando Galli-Bibiena** (1657–1743) who had abolished the symmetry and central perspective of the Renaissance stage in which, as Algarotti put it, 'giants dwindle by degrees as they come forward, and are dwarfed down to their native size, as they approach nearer to us'. (*Essay on Opera* 1755, English translation 1769, p.85). The reforms advocated by Algarotti had been anticipated in Paris in the 1720s by **Jean-Nicolas Servandoni** (1695–1766) who had been engaged at Covent Garden in 1749.

Though Garrick was receptive to these ideas about scenery it was not until 1771 that he engaged **Philip De Loutherbourg**.

Philip James De Loutherbourg (1740–1812)

Having studied and worked in Paris, De Loutherbourg came to London in 1771 and held the position of scenic designer at Drury Lane for ten years. De Loutherbourg introduced many innovations, several of them derived from Algarotti, in particular *chiaroscuro* lighting effects in which light was concentrated upon a particular part of the stage, such as a castle in moonlight, rather than being spread uniformly. He produced perspective on painted backdrops which he combined with practicable set pieces to achieve a new degree of illusion. For the 1779 pantomime *The Wonders of Derbyshire* or *Harlequin in the Peak* he visited the relevant locations such as the caverns at Castleton, and for O'Keeffe's 1785 pantomime *Omai* he used the sketches of the South Seas by John Webber who had accompanied Captain Cook on his last voyage:

> Loutherbourg planned the scenery. He had previously invented transparent scenery – moonshine, sunshine, fire volcanoes, etc as also breaking the scene into several pieces by the laws of perspective; showing miles and miles of distance.
>
> O'Keeffe, *Recollections*

After leaving Drury Lane, De Loutherbourg opened the Eidophusikon where he displayed scenic techniques (panoramas, backlighting and so on) for their own sake.

One of the most influential figures in the mid-eighteenth century French theatre was **Denis Diderot** (1713–84) whose interests ranged over philosophy, drama and acting. Though his own plays were not particularly successful examples of the *genre serieux* which he advocated, he did have more successful imitators, who explored the middle ground between comedy and tragedy in plays which were intended to turn the audience into better people. In *Paradoxe sur le Comedien* (*The Paradox of Acting*), published posthumously in 1830, Diderot contrasted carefully controlled repetitive acting with the unpredictable reliance on inspiration. An example of the former was **Claire Clairon** (1723–1803) who having 'by dint of hard work' got as near as possible to the concept was able 'to preserve that same nearness' by memory and practice, whereas her contemporary and rival **Marie Françoise Dumesnil** (1713–1803) 'comes on the stage without knowing what she is going to say, half the time she does not know what she is saying: but she has one sublime moment'. During his 1764 visit to Paris David Garrick saw and admired Mlle Clairon, but he also impressed Diderot and others with his advocacy of a more natural style of acting. When Garrick resumed his active management of Drury Lane he collaborated with **George Colman the Elder** (1732–94) on *The Clandestine Marriage* (1766) though he refused to play Lord Ogleby and a rift ensued between the two authors. In September 1769 (the wrong month, the wrong year) Garrick, at the invitation of the Stratford-upon-Avon town council, mounted the Shakespeare Jubilee in the dramatist's home town.

The Shakespeare jubilee

Appalling weather was partly responsible for the loss of £2,000 which Garrick attempted to recoup by re-staging the Stratford pageant at Drury Lane. Known as 'Shakespeare's priest' Garrick can be seen as the originator of 'bardolatry'. Though he still used Tate's *King Lear* and adapted *The Taming of the Shrew* as *Catherine and Petruchio* he did try to restore neglected plays such as *Antony and Cleopatra* to the stage. He was an assiduous collector of rare Shakespeare editions and left his collection to the British Museum. Shakespeare was effectively Drury Lane's house-dramatist with his plays accounting for nearly a third of the repertoire in some seasons. Eighteenth-century England was not a golden era for plays. As Cecil Price wrote 'Few new plays were acted, and the audiences' pleasure was derived from the repetition of plays they knew well.' (*Theatre in the Age of Garrick*, p.5).

Ironically it was to the century's greatest dramatist **Richard Brinsley Sheridan** (1751–1816) that Garrick sold his share of Drury Lane in 1776. On his death Garrick was buried in Westminster Abbey, a unique testimony to his personal distinction and his efforts on behalf of his profession. In contrast to the Hanoverians in Britain, other European royal houses actively promoted the theatre, none more so than King Gustavus IV of Sweden (1746–92) himself an actor and playwright.

The Drottningholm Court Theatre

Following a succession of temporary buildings, the first permanent theatre at the summer palace opened in 1754 and was burnt down in 1762. Charles Frederik Adelkrantz was commissioned to design a replacement, the original plans for which were over-ornate, but the theatre as completed in 1766 is an elegant house with a French neo-classical interior and a very deep stage in the Italian style with sophisticated machinery by

Donato Stopani. The theatre's heyday was the reign (1771–92) of Gustav IV who had it extended in 1791, but after his assassination the next year it fell into a timewarp until 1921. Drottningholm has survived, therefore, as a late example of Italian staging just as it was being superseded by Algarotti's innovations. It now hosts an annual summer season.

Richard Brinsley Sheridan (1751–1816)

His father (an actor) and mother (an authoress) sent Sheridan to Harrow School and intended him for the Law. At 21 he married Elizabeth Linley, the daughter of the composer, thereby providing himself with the material for *The Rivals* which was successfully staged in 1775 at Covent Garden, where his comic opera *The Duenna* followed later that year. By the time he completed *The School for Scandal* he controlled his own theatre, Drury Lane, where it was premiered in 1777, as was *A Trip to Scarborough*, his toned-down version of Vanbrugh's *The Relapse*. Though *The Critic* (1779) and *Pizarro* (1799) were to follow, Sheridan's energies were principally directed to management and politics – he became a Member of Parliament in 1780 and Secretary to the Treasury in 1783.

Oliver Goldsmith (1728–74) first made his mark in the theatre with *The Good Natured Man* at Covent Garden in 1768, which he followed in 1773 with *She Stoops to Conquer*. In his prologue to the latter Garrick wrote 'The Comic muse, long sick, is now a-dying!', an allusion to the dominance of so-called sentimental comedy with its conscious moralizing, its advocacy of virtue and the reform of the sinner. Leading exponents of sentimental comedy were Colley Cibber (*The Careless Husband* 1704) and Richard Steel (*The Conscious Lovers* 1722). In the prologue to *The Conscious Lovers* Leonard Welsted expressed the aspiration 'To chasten wit, and moralise the stage.'

An Essay on the Theatre

or

A Comparison between Laughing and Sentimental Comedy

… Comedy should excite our laughter by ridiculously exhibiting the Follies of the lower part of mankind … a new species of Dramatic

Composition has been introduced under the name of Sentimental
Comedy in which the virtues of Private Life are exhibited, rather
than the Vices exposed ... Humour at present seems to be departing
from the stage ...

Oliver Goldsmith, *Westminster Review*, January 1773

Theatres

Sentimental comedy's appeal was principally to the genteel middle-class
theatre-goer, but as the population of London increased so did the theatre-
going public: twenty-fold between 1737 and 1770 according to one
estimate. With Covent Garden and Drury Lane possessively guarding their
monopolies, their managers progressively extended their theatres. Garrick
had raised the capacity of Wren's Drury Lane to 2,000, but in 1791 the
theatre was condemned. The new theatre, designed by Henry Holland,
opened on 12 March 1794 and held 3,611. Covent Garden, which had been
rebuilt in 1787, was massively enlarged (also by Holland) in 1792. The

The interior of Covent Garden Theatre, c. 1763

proscenium arch of the 1794 Drury Lane was 13 m (43 feet) wide by 11.5 m (38 feet) high and behind it lay, in addition to elaborate stage machinery, four very large reservoirs of water and an iron curtain to cut off the auditorium from the stage. Fire was the scourge of the eighteenth-century theatre, relieved only partly by the introduction of gas lighting in 1817. Covent Garden was destroyed by fire in 1808 and Drury Lane in 1809. Covent Garden reopened in 1809, to designs by Robert Smirke, with a capacity of 3,000 and at a cost of £150,000. Drury Lane followed in 1812, to the designs of Benjamin Wyatt, with a capacity of 3,060 and at a cost of £400,000.

The effect of these larger theatres upon stage representation was considerable.

Richard Cumberland (1732–1811) Playwright

Since the stages of Drury Lane and Covent Garden have been so enlarged in their dimensions as to be henceforward theatres for spectators rather than playhouses for hearers, it is hardly to be wondered if their managers and directors encourage those representations to which their structure is best adapted ... (the) splendour of the scenes, the ingenuity of the machinist ... the rich display of dresses ... the captivating charms of the music, now in a great degree supersede the labours of the poet. There can be nothing very gratifying in watching the movements of an actor's lips, when we cannot hear the words that proceed from them ...

On the stage of old Drury in the days of Garrick the moving brow and penetrating eye of that matchless actor came home to the spectator ... upon the scale of modern Drury many of the finest touches of his art would of necessity fall short.

Memoirs, 1806, pp.57–8

The Kembles

The acting family (dynasty even) to whose lot it fell to lead their profession in the enlarged theatres of London was the Kembles. The paterfamilias was a provincial strolling player, previously a hair-dresser, **Roger Kemble** (1721–1802) whose marriage to **Sarah Ward** (d.1807) produced 12 children of whom the eldest was **Sarah** (1755–1831), the eldest son **John Philip** (1757–1822) and the youngest **Charles** (1775–1854).

John Philip Kemble

Although he had appeared on the stage as a child, John Philip was sent to Douai in France to train for the (Roman Catholic) priesthood. The lure of the theatre proved to be irresistible, but to it Kemble brought a severity and asceticism which may have been derived from his forsaken clerical calling. After pursuing his career in the provinces Kemble made his London debut at Hamlet at Drury Lane on 30 September 1783. Kemble's distinctive characteristics in the role were noted by his biographer James Boaden.

Kemble as Hamlet

He was of a solemn and deliberate temperament – his walk was always slow, and his expression of countenance contemplative – his utterance rather tardy for the most part, but always finely articulate … Mr Kemble played the part in a modern court dress of rich black velvet, with a star on the breast, the garter and pendant ribband of an order – mourning sword and buckles, with deep ruffles: the hair in powder; which, in the scene of feigned distraction, flowed dishevelled in front and over the shoulder.

Memoirs of the Life of John Philip Kemble, 1825, Vol 1, p.288

This image was captured by Sir Thomas Lawrence, for whom as for many eighteenth-century painters, the theatre was a favourite subject, but Shearer West has cited other illustrations of Kemble (as Coriolanus by Francis Peter Bourgeois for instance) which challenge 'the stereotypical picture of him as ever-dignified and ever-still'. (*The Image of the Actor*, p.73)

Whatever the degree of animation Kemble certainly set great store by the visual effects created on the stages of the two patent houses over both of which he presided during the course of his career. In 1794 Kemble engaged **William Capon** (1757–1827) whose scenery for *Macbeth* (21 April) included six chamber wings 'very elaborately studied from actual remains', a further step in the direction of antiquarianism begun by Macklin with his assumption of the 'old Caledonian habit' in 1774.

A full house at Drury Lane produced £700, but audience expectations were high and costs rose. Attractions such as the child prodigy **William Betty** (1791–1874), who was a sensation for a couple of seasons (1804–6) quickly faded. Kemble's choice of the Greek revivalist architect Robert Smirke for the rebuilding of Covent Garden in 1808 reflected the actor's classical style and his insistence upon the dignity of his art. His introduction of higher prices resulted in the Old Price Riots which continued for 67 nights. Kemble retired to Lausanne, Switzerland in 1817. Like Garrick he had assembled an impressive library, part of which was bought by the Duke of Devonshire.

Mrs Siddons (1755–1831)

Mrs Siddons – Sarah Kemble married Henry Siddons in 1773 – made her London debut for Garrick at Drury Lane in 1775, but was accounted such a failure that she returned to the provinces until 1782 when she took London by storm as Isabella in *The Fatal Marriage* (Southerne/Garrick). The improvement in Mrs Siddon's fortunes reflected not only her own talent but also the increasing importance of the provinces for her profession.

Provincial theatres

The provisions of the 1737 Licensing Act required provincial actors to exercise as much ingenuity as their metropolitan peers. Thus on 11 July 1774 Mrs Siddons, as a member of the Wolverhampton Company of Comedians, had appeared in a 'Concert of Vocal and Instrumental music' during the interval of which 'will be played (Gratis) the celebrated Comedy The West Indian'.

No town outside London could provide an audience for a theatre season of more than a few months; these were often associated with special occasions such as race meetings. Amongst the managers who prospered in the provinces **Tate Wilkinson** (1739–1803) was pre-eminent. From 1770 he ran a circuit of six theatres in the North of England, those in York and Hull having become Theatres Royal in 1769. Bath and Norwich were accorded royal patents in 1768, as were Liverpool (1771), Manchester (1775), Bristol (1778) and Newcastle (1788). In 1788 an Act was passed legalizing acting in the provinces and empowering magistrates to license acting companies. Two theatres survive from this period: the Theatre Royal, Bristol built in 1766 and the – smaller – Richmond Theatre, Yorkshire dating from 1788.

Mrs Siddons – as herself and in character – was the subject of paintings by Thomas Lawrence, Thomas Gainsborough, George Romney, Henry Fuseli and Joshua Reynolds whose *Mrs Siddons as the Tragic Muse* captured her at her most majestic. The dignity which she brought to tragic heroines was out of place in romantic comedy as was her over-insistence upon decorum in costume, nevertheless the emotional force which she brought to her acting is evident in this description of her in *As You Like It* by **Anna Seward** (1747–1809), the poet known as the 'Swan of Lichfield'.

Mrs Siddons as Rosalind at Lichfield 20 July 1786

The playful scintillation of colloquial wit, which most strongly mark that character, suit not the dignity of the Siddonian form and countenance. Her dress was injudicious … an ambiguous vestment, that seemed neither male nor female. [But when she says to Orlando 'To you I give myself – for I am *yours'*, she becomes] the whole soul of enamoured transport … that mistress of the passions.

H. Pearson, *The Swan of Lichfield*, 1936, p.91

When these qualities were applied to strong dramatic roles the effect was formidable. Mrs Siddons was at her most impressive as wife and mother, the former as Lady Macbeth and Mrs Beverley in Edward Moore's *The Gamester*; the latter as Constance in *King John* and Lady Randolf in John Home's *Douglas*. Audiences, critics and fellow actors all testified to Mrs Siddons's capacity to – in Macready's words – 'forget the actress in the character she assumed'. Her natural dignity, her sharp intelligence, her powerful vocal delivery and her passionate absorption in and projection of emotion ensure Mrs Siddon's place in the annals of great acting.

Mrs Siddons made her farewell appearance – as Lady Macbeth – on 29 June 1812, though she did subsequently appear in a benefit performance for her brother Charles and his wife on 9 June 1819.

The benefit

Mrs Barry is said to have been the first recipient of a benefit; by which the proceeds of a particular performance went to one or two members of the company. The incentive for the beneficiaries to drum up a large attendance is amusingly related by Charles Dickens in *Nicholas Nickleby*.

Dorothy Jordan (1761–1816)

Mrs Jordan was the antithesis of Mrs Siddons both on stage (where she excelled in comedy) and off (as the mistress of the Duke of Clarence by whom she had ten children). She was highly regarded as Viola (*Twelfth Night*) combining, in the view of Joshua Reynolds, 'feeling with sportive effect'. Her appearance, disguised as Cesario in a hussar's hat, was captured by John Hoppner, who painted several portraits of her.

Edmund Kean (1787/9–1833)

Kean's parentage and early life are cloaked in mystery. He was evidently something of an infant prodigy, becoming a proficient singer, dancer, fencer, acrobat and mimic. Between 1804 and 1814 Kean earned his living as a provincial actor, married (1808), fathered two sons, the elder dying in infancy, the younger, **Charles** (1811–68), following his father's profession after his education at Eton. Kean resisted the temptation of making his London debut prematurely, but when he did so as Shylock at Drury Lane on 26 January 1814 he became an overnight sensation. Replacing the conventional red beard with a black one Kean created a Shylock abounding in energy. Amongst the roles which he played in his first season were Richard III and Iago which confirmed his flair for malignity. It was Coleridge who observed of Kean that 'To see him act is like reading Shakespeare by flashes of lightning'.

In comparison with the classical nobility of Kemble, Kean captured the radical, romantic spirit of the age.

Leigh Hunt (1784–1859)

Grace exalts the person of Kean. In Kemble's handsomer figure it came to nothing, because it found nothing inside to welcome it. It received but 'cold comfort'. Kean's face is full of light and shade, his tones vary, his voice trembles, his eye glistens, sometimes with a tear: at least he can speak as if there were tears in his eyes, and he brings tears into those of other people.

The Tatler, 25 July 1831

Kean's personal life was as sensational as his performances. Following the court case arising from his affair with Charlotte Cox, whose husband was an Alderman and member of the Drury Lane committee, he was booed throughout his performance as Richard III. On 24 January 1825 Kean left

Edmund Kean as Richard III

for America, which he had already visited in 1820, but though he returned to the London stage the old magic had gone. His last appearance was at Covent Garden on 25 March 1833 as Othello to his son Charles's Iago. As he collapsed he moaned 'I am dying – speak to them for me'.

America

Kean was by no means the first English actor to seek refuge or fortune in America. The Puritan heritage of the early settlers was still rife. In 1687 Increase Mather had expressed alarm at 'much discourse of beginning Stage-Plays in New England'.

The distinction of being the first actor in America is accorded to **Anthony Aston** (c.1682–1753), the son of a well-to-do English family, who gave up the law for the stage and was performing in Charleston, South Carolina in 1703.

The New World's first theatrical dynasty was the Hallams, who encompassed a range of experience in the British theatre. **Lewis Hallam Snr** (1714–55/6) with his wife, family and 10 actors opened in Williamsburg, Virginia with *The Merchant of Venice* and *The Alchemist* on 15 September 1752. A temporary theatre had been built in Williamsburg as early as 1716 and other similar structures are recorded in New York (from 1732), Charleston (from 1736) and Philadelphia (from 1749). In 1756 the Hallams erected a theatre in Nassau Street, New York. Following the death of Lewis Hallam the enterprise was carried on by his son **Lewis Jnr** (c.1740–1808) and his widow who married **David Douglass** (?–1786). As in the English provinces where towns were not populous enough to support a permanent theatre, the players toured around the country.

The Southwark, erected in Philadelphia in 1766, is recognized as the first permanent theatre, although its appearance, in a print, suggests a meeting house with a bell tower. In contrast the Chestnut Street Theatre built in the same town in 1791 was modelled on the Theatre Royal, Bath. Other theatres followed in Baltimore, Boston and New York. Whatever the political effects of the Declaration of Independence (1776) the close links between the theatre in the United States and Britain were not severed, though inevitably a new tension was introduced.

Australia

The first manifestation of theatrical activity in Australia was the performance of Farquhar's *The Recruiting Officer* by convicts in Sydney on 4 June 1789. This is the subject of Timberlake Wertenbaker's play *Our Country's Good* (1988) based on the novel *The Playmaker* by Thomas Keneally. It was not until 1833 that a Theatre Royal was opened in Sydney.

The period from the early eighteenth century to the early nineteenth century shows very clearly how the theatre's progress is affected by the demands of its patrons, not only monarchs and aristocrats, but the population at large, as society (reflecting events in France as well as America) became increasingly democratic.

7 | VICTORIAN STAGES

Queen Victoria was already an enthusiastic theatre-goer when – aged 18 – she succeeded to the British throne in 1837 and, though she refrained from attending performances for 20 years after Prince Albert's death, her enchantment with the theatre was lifelong. During Victoria's lengthy (64 years) reign new opportunities opened up for the theatre from the densely populated towns and cities of industrial Britain to the new frontiers of the empire upon which the sun never set.

Reform

In 1832, as well as passing the Reform Bill, parliament turned its attention to the theatre through the Select Committee appointed to 'Inquire into the Laws affecting Dramatic Literature'. The Committee's report contained several recommendations of which the most significant were the abolition of the Patent Theatres' monopoly and the extension to playwrights of the legal protection enjoyed by other authors. The Dramatic Copyright Act was passed in 1833, but it was not until 1843 that the Theatre Regulation Act empowered all theatres to perform the legitimate drama. A leading member of the 1832 Select Committee was **Edward Bulwer Lytton** (1803–73) MP for St Ives, already a published novelist and a dramatist in the making. In *England and the English* (1833) Lytton recognized the need for entertainment amongst the new urban masses and considered the state's role in its provision.

England and the English

The physical condition of the Working Classes in manufacturing Towns is more wretched than we can bear to consider (vol.1, pp. 174–5). No! individual patronage is not advantageous to art, but there is a patronage which is – the patronage of the state ... (vol.2, p.176)

Edward Bulwer Lytton

Lytton upheld the example of France where the government supported the theatre and other arts. Although the Comédie-Français had lost its monopoly in 1791, Napoleon regarded it as an important national institution and in 1802 an annual subsidy was settled, initially 100,000 francs. Even during his Russian campaign Napoleon gave his attention to the Comédie-Français detailing its re-organization in the decree of Moscow (1812).

The case for establishing a National Theatre was made – by the radical politician, preacher and journalist W. J. Fox, amongst others – at the time of the abolition of the Patent Theatres' monopoly, but such a proposal was out of step not only with long-standing national tradition, but also the prevailing spirit of reform.

In England the onus for elevating the status of the theatre rested with the profession itself, which fortunately had in W. C. Macready a leader committed and equal to the task.

William Charles Macready (1793–1873)

Unusually for the son of actors Macready was sent to a major public school, Rugby, where he set his sights on a career in law. His father's financial difficulties necessitated not only the 15-year-old William's removal from Rugby, but also the boy's engagement, first as manager and then as actor, in the profession which he had been determined to avoid. In later life Macready expressed the opinion that 'In other callings the profession confers dignity on the initiated, on the stage the player must contribute respect by the exercise of his art.' Nevertheless Macready did not shirk the responsibility; after his debut as Romeo in Birmingham in 1810 he built up his experience and reputation in the provinces before – in 1816 – taking an engagement at Covent Garden as a counter-attraction to Edmund Kean at Drury Lane.

Macready's qualities as an actor were a dignified figure, an expressive face, a commanding voice and the intelligence to penetrate and express the psychological nature of his characters. His range was considerable, though comedy was not his real forte. He was an acclaimed Macbeth and Lear, and Virginius in Sheridan Knowles's play. Macready particularly admired the French actor **François Joseph Talma** (1763–1826) whom he saw perform in Paris in 1822 and seems to have adopted as a model.

Macready on Talma

Every turn and movement as he trod the stage might have given a model for the sculptor's art ... and yet [he seemed] utterly unconscious of the dignified and graceful attitudes he presented. His voice was flexible and powerful, and his delivery articulate to the finest point without a trace of pedantry ... Talma would dress some time before, and make the peculiarities of his costume familiar to him; at the same time that he thereby possessed himself more with the feeling of the character. I thought the practice so good, that I frequently adopted it and derived great benefit from it ...

Reminiscences, 1875, p.180

In 1826 Macready crossed the Atlantic and was warmly received in New York, Boston, Baltimore and Philadelphia. Amongst the American actors whom he saw and met socially was **Edwin Forrest** (1806–72) who in his turn undertook a European tour in 1834–6. These exchanges were not always conducive to cordial relationships and when Macready visited America for the third time in 1848 he encountered considerable hostility which Forrest had fomented. The cause was partly personal, but there was also a nationalistic element as the former colony sought to establish its own cultural identity. The climax came on 10 May 1849 with the Astor Place riots in which between 17 and 20 people died and many others were injured.

Macready's principal motive in visiting America was to replenish his funds, depleted by managerial losses, for retirement.

Although after the 1832 Select Committee's report the abolition of the Patent Theatres' monopoly was inevitable, before that took place (in 1843) Macready successively assumed the management of Covent Garden (1837–9) and Drury Lane (1841–3). Clearly Macready was not motivated by financial gain but, rather, the elevation of the theatre within the nation's cultural life. He extended the Shakespearean repertoire, ensuring full rehearsals and specially prepared sets and costumes for all his revivals, of which *King Lear* (25 January 1838) and *King John* (24 October 1842) were especially notable. He encouraged **Robert Browning** (1812–89), **Westland Marston** (1819–90) and **Sheridan Knowles** (1784–1862) to write plays. He also eschewed long runs even for popular productions and, though he brooked no rival, he ensured competence at least in his acting company. At a banquet in his honour on 19 June 1843 Macready proclaimed 'I aimed at elevating everything represented on the stage' and could rightly claim that through 'my attempts to redeem the Drama, I have secured some portion of public confidence'.

The two managers who could be regarded as Macready's heirs were Samuel Phelps and Charles Kean who, though they shared the goal of elevating the status of the theatre, pursued it in very different spheres.

Samuel Phelps (1804–78)

Phelps' early years in the provinces were followed by London engagements of which those with Macready seem to have been motivated by the senior actor's intention to restrict rather than encourage a talented newcomer. The abolition of the monopoly presented Phelps with an opportunity, but his choice of Sadler's Wells, best known for its large water tank on which sensational and spectacular melodramas were performed, was his own. In his public address to the residents of the unfashionable district of Islington Phelps proclaimed his intentions.

Phelp's address to the residents of Islington

Mrs Warner and Mr Phelps embarked their exertions in the management and performances of Sadler's Wells Theatre, in the hope of constantly rendering it what a theatre ought to be; a place for justly representing the works of our great dramatic poets ...

These circumstances [the abolition of the monopoly] justify the notion that each separate division of an immense metropolis, with its 2,000,000 inhabitants can have its own well-conducted theatre within a reasonable distance of the home of its patrons.

For the North of London, they offer an entertainment selected from the first stock drama in the world, reinforced by such novelties as can be produced by diligence and liberality ... and a Company of acknowledged talent ... These attractions are placed in a theatre where all can see and hear, and at a price fairly within the habitual means of all.

At Sadler's Wells Phelps was implementing the aspirations of the 1832 Select Committee and the 1843 Act, by enabling working folk in North London to experience (and enjoy) the finest dramatic fare at prices they could afford. Sadler's Wells contained an unusually high proportion of cheaper seats: 1,200 at 6d (2.5p) in the gallery and 1,000 at 1s (5p) in the pit. The top price was 3s (15p) in the dress circle and as his theatre's reputation grew Phelps attracted discerning playgoers from further afield – Charles Dickens for one.

During his 18-year tenure of Sadler's Wells Phelps staged 32 of Shakespeare's plays, including such rarities as *Timon of Athens* and *Pericles*, and also revived works by Massinger, Webster, Beaumont and Fletcher, though his record with new pieces was less impressive. The productions were carefully prepared with scenery and costumes appropriate to the play and the box-office income and a talented acting company capable of true ensemble work. As an actor in the Macready mould, Phelps acquitted himself equally well in comedy and tragedy. *A Midsummer Night's Dream* with its magical gauzes and dioramas and Phelps's self-important, but unexaggerated, Bottom was amongst his finest achievements.

Unlike many of his contemporaries Phelps did not venture to America, but in 1859 he took his company to Berlin where he enjoyed the patronage of the German royal family. Shakespeare's plays were to feature more prominently in the repertoires of German theatres than those of any other non-English speaking country.

Charles Kean (1811–68)

The Eton-educated son of the mercurial Edmund Kean, Charles claimed that 'if it had not been for my father's fame, I should have made my way with the public twice as easily.' True or not, Charles Kean with his rather expressionless face and monotonous nasal delivery was a very different actor from his father, though his admirers praised what they regarded as his natural style. **Ellen Tree** (1806–80), whom Charles married in 1842, was the more accomplished performer and her husband's staunch supporter in all he undertook.

In 1848 Charles Kean was appointed director of the Windsor Theatricals, Queen Victoria's and Prince Albert's initiative, in emulation of the royal courts of Europe, to raise the status of the theatre by their patronage. Though he scarcely commanded the esteem of his profession (Macready with his republican leanings was doubly resentful) Kean set about the task with characteristic conscientiousness and no small sense of his own importance. Queen Victoria extended her patronage to the Princess's Theatre in Oxford Street where, between 1850 and 1859, Kean drew a fashionable audience to his elaborate revivals of Shakespeare and the gentlemanly melodramas of **Dionysius Boucicault**.

Kean produced elaborate playbills in which he detailed the historical sources for the costumes, scenery and music with which he beguiled his audiences.

Charles Kean's playbill for *King Richard II* at the Princess's Theatre 1857

... An increasing taste for recreation wherein instruction is blended with amusement, has for some time been conspicuous in the English public; and surely, an attempt to render dramatic representations conducive to the diffusion of knowledge ... to surround the glowing imagery of the great Poet with accompaniments *true* to the time of which he writes ... *realising* the scenes and actions which he describes ... exhibiting men as they once lived ... can scarcely detract from the enduring influence of his genius. Repeated success justifies the conviction that I am acting in accordance with the general feeling. When plays, which formerly commanded but occasional repetition, are enabled, by no derogatory means, to attract audiences for successive months, I cannot be wrong in presuming that the course I have adopted is supported by the irresistible force of public opinion, expressed in the suffrage of an overwhelming majority.

His hyperbole not withstanding, with prices at 5s (25p) in the dress circle, Kean's 'overwhelming majority' consisted principally of the well-to-do and his lavish productions required long runs to recover their investment. Nevertheless it must be acknowledged that Charles Kean caught the mood of the new, educated, playgoer in the decade of the Great Exhibition, the Pre-Raphaelite Brotherhood and the popularization of photography.

Kean was elected a Fellow of the Society of Antiquaries in 1857, but the knighthood, like the financial rewards, which he and Ellen thought was his due was not forthcoming and the Keans set off on a gruelling tour of Australia, New Zealand and America. In the antipodes they were indeed theatrical pioneers and the tercentenary of Shakespeare's birth found the couple in Melbourne where they performed acts from four different Shakespeare plays.

The Shakespeare tercentenary of 1864

In *On Heroes, Hero-Worship and the Heroic in History* (1841) Thomas Carlyle had hailed Shakespeare as 'the grandest thing we have yet done. For our honour among foreign nations, [and] as an ornament to our

English household'. The Shakespeare tercentenary provided the opportunity for England to celebrate her cultural superiority over other nations, but it also exposed the tensions within English society. London, as the capital, competed with Stratford-upon-Avon, the birthplace; working men's movements in both places challenged their social superiors' claims on Shakespeare both for their own purposes and as the arbiters of taste for the lower orders and, not surprisingly, the theatre tried to enhance its own status by appropriating the bard for itself.

In Stratford-upon-Avon, under **Edward Flower**'s (1805–83) strong leadership, an impressive and versatile – albeit temporary – pavilion was erected, the forerunner of the first Shakespeare Memorial Theatre – opened in 1879 and now the Swan Theatre – and the 1932 building which is the Royal Shakespeare Company's principal stage.

Playwrights

Shakespeare, whose plays had to be shortened, rearranged and even rewritten to fit them for the Victorian stage, was not an apt model for aspiring dramatists many of whom, nevertheless – mistakenly – adopted his structures and style. Pre-eminent amongst neo-Elizabethans was **James Sheridan Knowles** who, despite having been born in Cork, was frequently referred to as a latterday Shakespeare.

For a play to take its place in the national dramatic canon it has to combine literary distinction with theatrical effectiveness. With the ever-increasing number of theatres consequent upon the 1843 legislation the demand for plays was massive and the supply ranged from burletta to vaudeville with – in Allardyce Nicoll's estimation – over 70 designations in between. Few pieces from this huge output have survived into the modern repertoire.

Melodrama

The dominant form of the period, melodrama, spawned numerous varieties: Gothic, Eastern, military, nautical and domestic. **Douglas Jerrold**'s (1803–57) *Black-Eyed Susan*, which combined the nautical and the domestic, sustained its popularity from its premiere at the Surrey Theatre on 8 June 1829 with **T. P. Cooke** (1786–1864) as the hero William to **William Terriss**'s (1847–97) celebrated assumption of the role at the Adephi Theatre on 23 December 1896.

Pantomime

Pantomime became established as an integral part of the Victorian Christmas. **J. R. Planché** (1796–1880), **E. L. Blanchard** (1820–89) and **H. J. Byron** (1834–84), all of whom wrote successful pantomimes, were also distinguished in other fields: Planché as an authority on heraldry and author of *A History of British Costume* (1834); Blanchard as a journalist and editor of Shakespeare; Byron as the scribe of 150 plays of which *Our Boys* ran for 1,362 performances (1 January 1875–18 April 1879). In the 1850s the hero became the principal boy with **Madame Céleste** (1810/1–82) generally acknowledged as the prototype. In the 1880s and 1890s **Augustus Harris Jnr** (1851–96) turned Drury Lane into the home of spectacular pantomime engaging popular music hall artistes such as **Marie Lloyd** (1870–1922) and **Dan Leno** (1860–1904) as speciality acts.

Music-hall

The origins of music-hall lay in public house entertainment. The 1843 Theatres Act rested responsibility for such places with the local magistrates rather than the Lord Chamberlain. The first purpose-built music-hall was the Canterbury in Lambeth (1852). In due course theatres – under the jurisdiction of the Lord Chamberlain – were built specifically for the performance of music-hall, several of them the work of the distinguished architect **Frank Matcham** (c.1854–1920). Managers such as **Oswald Stoll** (1866–1942) and **Edward Moss** (1854–1912) ran lucrative circuits capitalizing on the popularity of such stars as **Marie Lloyd**, **Albert Chevalier** (1862–1923), **Dan Leno**, **Vesta Tilley** (1864–1952) and **George Robey** (1869–1954).

Some pioneer playwrights

Dionysius Lardner Boucicault (1820–90) is credited with 150 to 200 plays ranging from his early success *London Assurance* (1841) in the comedy of manners tradition to his gentlemanly melodramas *The Corsican Brothers* (1852) for Charles Kean and from his sensational *The Poor of New York* (1857) to his influential Irish plays, *The Colleen Bawn* (1860), *Arrah-na-Pogue* (1864) and *The Shaughraun* (1874). As an actor, manager and playwright Boucicault's career was truly international. The impulse was often the need to escape from a tight corner, but this led to initiatives such as the campaign for new copyright laws in the United States.

Tom Taylor (1817–80), Professor of English Literature, barrister, senior civil servant and editor of *Punch*, wrote over 70 plays. *Our American Cousin* (1858) was his greatest success thanks largely to **Edward Sothern**'s (1826–81) performance as the imbecile Lord Dundreary, but *The Ticket-of-Leave Man* (1863), with its detective Hawkshaw and wronged 'Lancashire Lad', Robert Brierly has proved to be his most durable and influential work.

Charles Reade (1814–84), Oxford don and novelist, wrote *Masks and Faces* (1852), a play about Peg Woffington and David Garrick, with Taylor. His depiction of prison life in *It's Never Too Late To Mend* (1854) broke new ground as did *Drink* (1879) his version of Zola's *L'Assommoir*.

Tom Robertson (1829–71), the eldest of 22 children of an actor, together with many of his siblings, made youthful apperances with their father's company. During the 1860s Robertson pioneered the new domestic – 'teacup and saucer' – comedies of which *Caste* (1867) is still occasionally revived. Pinero's *Trelawny of the 'Wells'* (1898) includes an affectionate portrait of Robertson as the aspiring playwright Tom Wrench.

The Bancrofts

The success of Robertson's plays owed much to the care and attention lavished upon them by the Bancrofts (**Squire Bancroft** 1841–1926 and his wife **Marie** 1839–1921 née Wilton) who renovated the Prince of Wales's Theatre in 1865 and attracted a 'respectable' clientele to the plays of Robertson, which were staged realistically with box sets. Squire Bancroft was knighted in 1897.

The Kendals

Another leading theatrical couple were Robertson's sister Madge and her husband **William Kendal** (1843–1917), whose management of the Haymarket Theatre was distinguished with the premieres of **W. S. Gilbert**'s (1836–1911) *The Palace of Truth* (1870), *Pygmalion and Galatea* (1871), *The Wicked World* (1873) and *Charity* (1874), prior to his celebrated partnership with **Sir Arthur Sullivan** (1842–1900). Ever the *grande dame* off-stage and on, **Madge Kendal** (1848–1935) was appointed DBE in 1926.

During 1864 T. W. Robertson contributed a series of articles on 'Theatrical Types' to the *Illustrated Times* which provide colourful vignettes of contemporary theatre folk and their way of life.

Tom Robertson's Theatrical Types – Varieties of Managers

The Commercial Manager is a very common type ... He is a great man for bargains, and will buy a quantity of damaged velvets for a fabulously small sum, after which he will search for an author to write him a piece for the velvets 'Lovely velvets – make any piece popular them velvets would,' says the Commercial Manager. The drama found, if it fail he despairs of the prospects of the theatre. Publics are so fickle nowadays. 'Who would have thought that with them velvets any piece could fail?'

The Scene Painter

The scene-painter is usually one of the pleasantest men in the theatre ... It is a great power the theatrical scene-painter holds between his pliant thumb and fingers. He copies nature on a large scale ...

In these present days of scenic display, when even no poor ghost can walk undisturbed by scientific satellites, lime-lights, mirrors and the like, the Scene-painter is a far more important person in the theatre than the Tragedian ...

Scenery

The nineteenth century was the era of the picture-frame stage ... in 1880 Squire Bancroft literally encased all four sides of the Haymarket Theatre's proscenium arch in a picture frame. Throughout the period a succession of scenic artists deployed their talents and the new technologies available to them to produce ever more elaborate and convincing realizations of life past and present. The precedence between historical/geographical accuracy and theatrical effectiveness was hotly contested for costumes as well as scenery.

As already noted, an early exponent of antiquarianism was **William Capon** at Drury Lane for J. P. Kemble. In 1823 Charles Kemble proved himself to be a more thorough-going antiquarian when he engaged **J. R. Planché** for the costumes in *King John*. **Clarkson Stanfield** (1793–1867), an admired marine artist who was elected to the Royal Academy in 1835, perfected the diorama for Macready's *Henry V* in 1839 at Drury Lane. Meanwhile at Covent Garden the **Grieves** had established themselves dynastically.

Thomas Grieve (1799–1882), **Frederick Lloyds** (1818–94), **William Gordon** (1801–74) and **J. Dayes** executed the triumphs of antiquarianism which were the hallmark of Charles Kean's management at the Princess's Theatre. Scenes such as the interpolated 'Historical Episode' in *King Richard II* combined substantial scenery with painted cloths, using the diagonal of the stage to create maximum scope for the procession which concluded with the appearance – on horseback– of 'the deposed and captive King, Richard the Second'. Several members of Kean's scenic team worked for **Charles Calvert** (1828–79) at the Prince's Theatre, Manchester where from 1864 until 1875 he advanced the antiquarian cause in revivals such as *Henry V* (1871) with its tableau of the Battle of Agincourt and, in emulation of Kean, its 'Historical Episode Reception of King Henry the Fifth on Entering London after the Battle of Agincourt'. Calvert's *Henry V* was transported to Booth's Theatre, New York in 1875 with **George Rignold** (1839–1912) in the title role and was subsequently toured across America and Australia, returning to London in 1879.

By then **Henry Irving** had assumed the management of the Lyceum Theatre where his scene painters included **Hawes Craven** (1837–1910), **W. L. Telbin** (1846–1931) and, later, **Joseph Harker** (1855–1927). Irving often engaged Royal Academicians – Burne Jones, Ford Madox Ford, Seymour Lucas and Alma-Tadema – as advisers and/or designers. Irving was less concerned about historical accuracy, striving above all for unity between all the elements to express the mood of the play. Herbert Beerbohm Tree's scenic team included Joseph Harker and **Walter Hann** (1837–1922), but the taste for monumentalism on stage was ebbing when they produced *Julius Caesar* to Alma-Tadema's designs in 1898.

Lighting

Scenery was closely related to, and dependent upon, lighting. At the Lyceum, which had been the first theatre to be illuminated by gas, Irving introduced the practice of extinguishing the auditorium lights during the performance, but would have no truck with electricity with which the Savoy Theatre was equipped in 1881. Irving, who employed 30 gasmen and 8 limelight operators, conducted extensive lighting rehearsals without

Behind the scenes at the play, nineteenth century

any actors present. Irving achieved his most spectacular lighting effect in the Brocken Scene in *Faust*. Though Henry James cared nothing for 'the spurting flames' and the 'importunate limelight', ordinary playgoers were enraptured.

The Brocken scene in *Faust*

Mephistopheles summoned his spirits once more, and the mad dancing briefly resumed. Thunder rolled again; the red glasses of twenty-five limelights shining through the background and upon openings in the rocks from which steam rose conveyed the impression that earth and sky were aflame. The rocks became molten and a rain of fire fell from the sky …

Michael Booth, *Victorian Spectacular Theatre*, p.120

Henry Irving (1838–1905)

Henry Irving overcame many disadvantages – humble origins, methodist upbringing, gangling figure and mannered voice – to become artistically, professionally and socially the undisputed leader of his profession. He served a long and testing apprenticeship in the provinces, beginning in Sunderland in 1856 and it was not until he persuaded **Hezekiah Bateman** (1812–75) to stage *The Bells* at the Lyceum Theatre in 1871 that he achieved metropolitan success.

In 1878, with Ellen Terry as his leading lady, Irving assumed the management of the Lyceum Theatre where during the next two decades, he created a National Theatre in all but name, receiving the reward of a knighthood in 1895.

As an actor, Irving had stern critics, foremost amongst whom was **George Bernard Shaw**, who wrote for *The Saturday Review* during the 1890s. Irving described his approach to acting as follows: 'There are two ways of portraying a character on the stage, either you can try to turn yourself into that person – which is impossible – or, and this is the way to act, you can take that person and turn him into yourself. That is how I do it.' Many of Irving's finest creations were conscience-stricken, remorseful men: the guilt-ridden murderer Mathias in *The Bells*, W. G. Wills's Eugene Aram, Sir Edward Mortimer in Colman's *The Iron Chest* and, of course, Macbeth. He ranged from the demonic (Mephistopheles in *Faust*) to the saintly (Tennyson's Becket), always conveying the character's inner psychological and spiritual life.

Henry Irving as Mathias in *The Bells*

Edward Gordon Craig on *The Bells*

The thing Irving set out to do was to show us the sorrow which slowly and remorselessly beat him down. As, no matter who the human being may be, and what his crime, the sorrow which he suffers must appeal to our hearts, so Irving set out to wring our hearts, not to give us a clever exhibition of antics such as a murderer would be likely to go through. He does not appeal to any silly sentimentality in you – he merely states the case by showing you that quite obviously here is a strong human being who, through a moment of weakness, falls into error and becomes for two hours a criminal – does what he knows he is doing – acts deliberately – but (and here is Irving) acts automatically, as though impelled by an immense force, against which no resistence is possible.

Henry Irving, 1930, pp.57–8

Ellen Terry (1847–1928)

Edward Gordon Craig (1872–1966) and his sister **Edy** (1869–1947) were Ellen Terry's children by the architect and theatrical designer **E. W. Godwin** (1833–86) with whom she lived for seven years following the breakdown of her youthful (at only 16) marriage to the artist **G. F. Watts** (1817–1904). Ellen Terry, who came from a theatrical family, made her debut as Mamillius in Charles Kean's revival of *The Winter's Tale* in 1856. The subject of portraits by Watts ('Choosing', 'Ophelia'), Graham Robertson and John Singer Sargent and photographs by Lewis Carroll, Ellen Terry was the embodiment of young English womanhood, innately feminine, delicately lady-like, tender, graceful, spontaneous and essentially innocent. At the Lyceum her Shakespearean roles included: Ophelia, Juliet, Desdemona, Lady Macbeth, Cordelia, Portia, Imogen and Volumnia. Her casting as Volumnia to Irving's Coriolanus reflected the fact that the decisive factor in the Lyceum repertoire was Irving's – not Ellen Terry's – role.

Ellen Terry became a DBE (Dame of the British Empire) in 1925. Her three sisters and brother all went on the stage and the family tradition was upheld by **John Gielgud** (b. 1904).

Irving's flair as a producer has already been illustrated with reference to scenery and lighting, but however elaborate these were he always regarded them as subsidiary to acting – his own at least. The scale of the Lyceum operation was vast – the payroll for *Robespierre* (1899) totalled 639; 355 of them performers and musicians, 236 on the technical side and 48 administrators. Audiences included the most elevated (the Prince of Wales), the post powerful (Gladstone and Disraeli) and the most gifted (Oscar Wilde) in the land.

Irving was regarded within and outside the theatre as its leader, a role he fulfilled as fervently as any on the stage. Whether he was addressing the Church of England Temperance Society (March 1876) or the Royal Academy Banquet (May 1891) he proclaimed the theatre as a force for social and educational good in the nation and the lives of its people.

Although there was a financial motive behind his eight North American tours, Irving undoubtedly saw himself as a cultural ambassador for his country. His final years were spent mainly in the English provinces and he died in Bradford after a performance as Becket ('Into Thy hands, O Lord – into Thy hands!'), but he was honoured with a funeral and burial in Westminster Abbey.

The era of the actor-manager

The model for success in the Victorian theatre was the (usually male) actor-manager who ran his own theatre, produced and starred in most of the plays alongside his leading lady, who may or may not have been his wife. Several of these actor-managers were former members of Irving's Lyceum company:

William Terriss (1847–1897) appeared as Claudio (*Much Ado About Nothing*) King Henry VIII, Edgar and Henry II (in *Becket*) with Irving at the Lyceum. He subsequently established himself at the Adelphi outside the stage door of which he was assassinated by an out-of-work actor Richard Archer Prince on 16 December 1897.

George Alexander (1858–1918) after experience with Irving and the Kendals, was lessee and manager of the St James's Theatre (1891–1918) where he cultivated new plays (by Pinero, Wilde, Galsworthy) and a fashionable audience. He was knighted in 1911.

Johnston Forbes-Robertson (1853–1937), his Lyceum roles included Buckingham (*Henry VIII*); he was much admired as Hamlet by Shaw in whose *The Devil's Disciple* and *Caesar and Cleopatra* he enjoyed great success. Married to the American actress **Gertrude Elliott** (1874–1950). Knighted in 1913.

John Martin-Harvey (1863–1944). Though his opportunities during his 14 years at the Lyceum were limited, he achieved long-running success with *The Only Way*. Worked with Reinhardt on *Oedipus Rex* (1912). Partnered by his wife **Nina de Silva** (1869–1949). Knighted 1921.

Frank Benson (1858–1939) made his professional debut with Irving in1882 having gained Ellen Terry's praise for his performances with OUDS (Oxford University Dramatic Society), but he soon set up his own company, touring principally Shakespeare, with regular seasons in Stratford. His wife **Constance** (1860–1946) was an actress. Knighted 1916.

Though never members of the Lyceum company, other leading actor-managers were:

Herbert Beerbohm Tree (1853–1917) made an early impression as the Revd Robert Spalding in **Charles Hawtrey**'s (1858–1923) farce *The Private Secretary* (1884). He entered management at the Comedy Theatre (1887) and after nine years at the Haymarket (1887–96) opened Her Majesty's which had been designed for him by **C. J. Phipps** (1835–97) and which he managed until 1915. A compelling, if erratic, character actor, Tree's repertoire included Shakespeare, Wilde, Ibsen, Shaw and Stephen Phillips. His wife **Maud** (1863–1937) partnered him on stage until their personal relationship became strained by Tree's numerous extra-marital affairs. He was knighted in 1917.

Charles Wyndham (1837–1919) specialized in contemporary drama, especially the plays of H. A. Jones. In 1899 he built the theatre which still bears his name. His second wife was **Mary Moore** (1869–1931), the widow of the dramatist **James Albery** (1838–89); after Wyndham's death she continued in the management of his theatre.

Management was not an entirely male preserve.

Lillie Langtry (1852–1929), the daughter of the Dean of Jersey, made her debut in 1881 as Kate Hardcastle in *She Stoops to Conquer*; in private life her conquests already included the Prince of Wales. Though never regarded as a great actress she was a competent manager running her own company in London, the provinces and the United States.

Mrs Patrick Campbell's (1865–1940) most celebrated roles were Pinero's Paula in *The Second Mrs Tanqueray* (1893) and Eliza Doolittle in

Shaw's *Pygmalion* (1914). Her attempts to continue her career in later life were not successful.

Most of the leaders of the theatrical profession at the end of the nineteenth century came from non-theatrical backgrounds, attracted to the stage by its new respectability and the substantial financial rewards which it offered. Michael Booth cites the example of **John Hare** (1844–1921) who received £5 a week for playing Sam Gerridge in *Caste* in 1867 and was offered £100 to play the same part in 1889 (*Theatre in the Victorian Age*, 1991, p.119).

Although London was the hub of the nation's theatre, the expanding network of railways made extensive tours both possible and, potentially, highly profitable.

The new wave

The attitudes and achievements of actor-managers towards the up-and-coming generation of dramatists was variable. Shaw repeatedly berated Irving for his failure to espouse the 'New Drama', but to no avail. Later Shaw had more success with Forbes-Robertson and Tree, who also staged Wilde, as did George Alexander.

H. A. Jones (1851–1929). Following the success of his superior melodrama *The Silver King* (1882), of which Matthew Arnold wrote 'But in general throughout the piece the diction and sentiments are natural, they have sobriety and propriety, they are literature', Jones directed his efforts to writing plays of substance with literary quality, such as *Michael and his Lost Angel* (1896) and *The Liars* (1897). He advanced his ideas about the theatre in *The Renaissance of the English Drama* (1895).

A. W. Pinero (1855–1934) worked as an actor for ten years. His plays can be grouped into farces (*The Magistrate* 1886, *Dandy Dick* 1887) and serious social dramas (*The Second Mrs Tanqueray* 1893). In *Trelawny of the 'Wells'* (1898) he recaptured the lost theatre of the 1860s. He was knighted in 1909.

Oscar Wilde (1854–1900). Some apprentice pieces and *Salomé* (banned in England, produced in Paris by Sarah Bernhardt in 1894) notwithstanding, Wilde's reputation as a dramatist rests on his four plays in the comedy of manners tradition: *Lady Windermere's Fan* (1892), *A Woman of No Importance* (1893), *An Ideal Husband* (1895) and *The Importance of Being Earnest* (1895).

G. B. Shaw (1856–1950) was a devotee of **Barry Sullivan** (1821–91) during his early theatre-going in Dublin. He learnt his craft with six, unsuccessful, novels and music and drama criticism. He collaborated with the Ibsen translator **William Archer** (1856–1924) on *Widower's House* which was staged in 1892 by **J. T. Grein's** (1862–1935) Independent Theatre which staged 'non-commerical work'. *You Never Can Tell* was produced in 1899 by the Stage Society which was also dedicated to 'minority' drama and continued its work until 1930. It was at the Royal Court Theatre under the joint management of **John Vedrenne** (1863–1930) and **Harley Granville Barker** (1877–1946) that Shaw established his reputation with *John Bull's Other Island* (1904) and later plays.

Queen Victoria's reign was highly propitious for the theatre in Britain and not without benefits for other countries. Encouraged by her patronage, liberated by government legislation, facilitated by technological advances – not least in transport – enfranchised by the inhabitants of the growing industrial conurbations, challenged by the new frontiers of colonization, the theatre enjoyed a period of unexampled prosperity and expansion, reflected in the increase in the membership of the profession between the census of 1841 (1,463) and 1901 (12,487). The period produced many fine actors from Macready to Irving and eventually some important dramatists, but the long-awaited emergence of literary drama brought with it the segregation of art and entertainment, with the mass of the population seeking its pleasures elsewhere than in the theatre.

8 | EUROPEAN VOICES

From its early days the theatre had crossed national frontiers but during the second half of the nineteenth century it did so with increasing rapidity and ease. In 1871 Thomas Cook and Sons organized a 'package tour' to the Passion Play in Oberammergau. Preceding decennial productions had attracted numerous independent English visitors and by the end of the century **Shaw**, **Frank Harris** (1856–1931) and **Jerome K. Jerome** (1859–1927) had all made the pilgrimage. Not that all was plain sailing; the 1870 performances of the Passion Play having been suspended because of the Franco-Prussia War.

Germany

The European country with which Britain was most closely associated was, of course, Germany with the royal family consolidating links through the marriage of Prince Albert's and Queen Victoria's eldest daughter to William of Prussia who, was proclaimed Emperor of, a united, Germany at Versailles on 18 January 1871, just days before Paris capitulated to his forces. Of the heads of the many small territories which made up the new united Germany **Georg II** (1826–1914), the **Duke of Saxe-Meiningen** was content to devote himself principally to the Court theatre, which, although it had opened in 1831, had made little impact beyond the small town with its 8,000 inhabitants.

The Meiningen Players

Prior to becoming Duke, Georg had received a broad education and travelled widely taking every opportunity to attend theatrical performances of which those in Berlin by **Ludwig Tieck** (1773–1853) and in London by Charles Kean impressed him most. Ludwig Tieck, an enthusiastic and knowledgeable Shakespearian, was instrumental in the completion of **A. W. Schlegel**'s (1767–1845) translation of the plays and in 1843 produced

A Midsummer Night's Dream on an Elizabethan-style stage. From 1870–95 Duke Georg was the *Intendant* (Chief Administrator) of his own theatre which enjoyed its golden age during 1873–91 under **Ludwig Chronegk** (1837–91) as *regisseur* (director) with **Ellen Franz** (1839–1923), the Duke's third wife, completing the directorate.

Rehearsals customarily took place in the evening when the Duke had completed his state duties. From the outset the full stage set was used and the actors were required to perform – not simply read through – their roles. The company, which numbered 70, had no stars and the extras, of which there could be as many as 200, were divided into small groups to rehearse before being brought together as a single unit. The opening night of a production was not announced until the Duke was fully satisfied with it; only two performances a week took place during a season of six months. Shakespeare figured prominently in the repertoire followed by Schiller, but Ibsen's *Ghosts* was produced in 1886–7. At Chronegk's suggestion the Meiningen company toured throughout Europe, giving over 2,500 performances between 1874 (Berlin) and 1890 (Russia). Amongst those who attended were **Konstantin Stanislavsky** (1863–1938) in Moscow and **André Antoine** (1858–1943) in Paris.

Stanislavsky on Chronegk

Outside of the theatre Kronek's [sic] relations even with the third-rate actors of his company were simple and friendly. He even seemed to flaunt this simplicity of conduct. But as soon as a rehearsal began and Kronek mounted his usual place, he would be reborn …

The restraint and cold-bloodedness of Kronek were to my taste and I wanted to imitate him. With time I also became a despotic stage director. Very soon the majority of Russian stage directors began to imitate me in my despotism as I imitated Kronek. There was a whole generation of despotic stage directors, who, alas, did not have the talents of Kronek or of the Duke of Meiningen … Only with time, as I began to understand the wrongness of the principle of the director's despotism, I valued that good which the Meiningen Players brought us, that is, their director's methods for showing the spiritual contents of the drama …

In the life of our Society and especially in me the Meiningen Players created a new and important period.

My Life in Art, 1924, 1967 edn. pp.191–3

André Antoine on the Meiningen Company, July 1888

... the Meininger achieve ensemble scenes that are extraordinarily lifelike ... that fitting use of full-back positions contributes greatly to the actor's conviction and the spectator's illusion ... The mechanics of stage groupings is capitally perfected.

Observe that I am not at all, so to speak, carried away by them. Their discordant settings, oddly erected, are infinitely less well-painted than ours. They overdo the use of practicables, putting them everywhere. The costumes, splendid and ridiculously rich when they are strictly historical, are almost always in bad taste when, there being no documentary evidence, imagination and originality must be employed. Their lighting effects are very successful, but so often they are regulated without art ...

Also, after an extraordinary torrential rain, obtained by means of projections, I was disturbed to see the water stop abruptly, instead of letting up slowly.

from Adolphe Thalasso, *Le Théâtre Libre*, 1909, p.166

Richard Wagner (1813–83)

From a theatrical family, Richard Wagner turned to music early and he completed his first opera *Die Feen* at 18. The four operas making up *The Ring of the Nibelung* were composed over a period of more than 20 years, receiving their first complete performance in 1876 when the Festspielhaus at Bayreuth opened. Wagner's opera house, to the design of which several architects and scene designers contributed, was in marked contrast to Bayreuth's existing Margave's Opera House of 1748 – in the rococo style by the Italian Bibiena family. The auditorium of the Festspielhaus was fan-shaped accommodating 1,345 in 30 rows of stepped seats in the raked stalls with a further 100 in a box at the rear and 300 in the balcony. Instead of the traditional tiers of boxes enforcing the social segregation of the audience Wagner created a classless theatre in which the same price was charged for all seats. A curved wall in front of the sunken orchestra pit served to conceal it from the audience and direct sound beneath the stage.

The stage, which lay behind a double proscenium arch, was traditional, but on it Wagner, librettist and composer, aspired towards *Gesamtkuntswerk* (complete art work) in which music, language and setting were brought

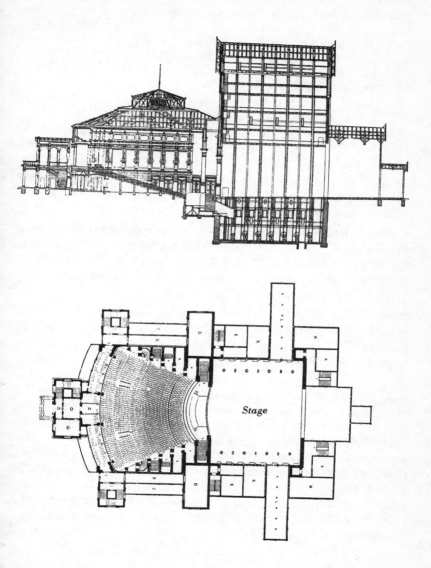

Stage

Interior of the Wagner's Festspielhaus at Bayreuth, 1876

into complete harmony in the service of total illusionism rather than realism. Wagner's ideas were further developed by **Adolphe Appia** (1862–1928) and **Edward Gordon Craig**.

German dramatists

Nineteenth-century Germany produced a number of innovative dramatists:

Georg Buchner (1813–37) medic and revolutionary whose small dramatic output – *Danton's Death* (1835), *Leonce and Lena* (1836) and *Woyzech* (1837) – had far-reaching effects, not least on **Bertolt Brecht**.

Frank Wedekind (1864–1918) is now best known for *Spring Awakening*, his controversial exploration of puberty (1891, performed 1906). He also influenced Brecht especially in his use of episodic structure.

Gerhardt Hauptmann (1862–1946) was an exponent of naturalism on the principles of Henrik Ibsen and Émile Zola. His first play *Before Dawn* (1889) was produced at the Freie Bühne which **Otto Brahm** (1856–1912) had established in Berlin in imitation of Antoine's Théâtre Libre. Later plays included *The Weavers* (1892).

Arthur Schnitzler (1862–1931) an Austrian doctor who knew Freud and with whom he shared a fascination with psychology and unconscious motives which he explored in *Reigen/La Ronde* (1890) and *Liebelei/The Game of Love* (1895).

Naturalism/Realism

In the context of the late nineteenth century, naturalism had two meanings: the exploration of natural causes, heredity/environment, on character and behaviour; and the accurate reproduction of the surface details of life on stage (and in paintings). Realism is often used interchangedly with naturalism, but more precisely it is the reality of human experience which, though it can be represented by the concrete and physical, can also be an expression of internal consciousness.

France

Throughout the nineteenth century the English theatre relentlessly translated, adapted, plagiarized and imitated French drama.

Mr. Vincent Crummles, theatre manager, to Nicholas Nickleby

'Do you understand French?'

'Perfectly well.'

'Very good,' said the manager, opening the table-drawer and giving a roll of paper from it to Nicholas. 'There! Just turn that into English and put your name on the tilt-page. Damn me,' said Mr Crummles angrily, 'if I haven't often said that I wouldn't have a man or woman in my company that wasn't master of the language, so that they might learn it from the original, and play it in English and by that means save all this trouble and expense.'

Nicholas smiled, and pocketed the play.

Charles Dickens, *Nicholas Nickleby*, 1838–9

Auguste Eugène Scribe (1791–1861) was immensely prolific (over 300 plays) and versatile. He was most celebrated for the one-act *vaudeville* and as the originator of the well-made play, in which events were manipulated to create suspense leading to some startling development just before the end of each act. Other exponents of the well-made play were **Émile Augier** (1820–89); **Eugène Labiche** (1815–88) and – in farce – **Georges Feydeau** (1862–1921).

Alexandre Dumas père (1802–70) and his son **Alexandre Dumas fils** (1824–95) were both successful dramatists. Père's speciality was historical dramas with subjects ranging from Napoleon to the English actor Edmund Kean; fils made his name with *La Dame aux Camélias* (written 1848, performed 1852), a sympathetic treatment of a 'kept woman' in contemporary Paris, and thereby established the woman-with-a-past as a prime subject for the next 50 years or so. Though he adopted many of the devices of the well-made play Dumas fils developed a greater degree of realism.

Victorien Sardou (1831–1908) wrote both large-scale historical dramas including several vehicles (*La Tosca* 1887, *Cléopâtre* 1890 and *Gismonda* 1894) for **Sarah Bernhardt** (1844–1923) and contemporary social comedies such as *Divorçons/Let's Get a Divorce* (1880) to all of which he brought his considerable skills in stagecraft and – as director – consummate romantic realism.

Not everyone was persuaded.

G. B. Shaw at *Fedora* Herman Merivale's (1839–1906) English version of Sardou's play at the Haymarket Theatre, 25 May 1895 and *Gismonda* at Daly's Theatre, 27 May 1895

Up to this day week I had preserved my innocence as a playgoer sufficiently never to have seen Fedora. Of course I was not altogether new to it, since I had seen Diplomacy Dora, and Theodora, and La Toscadora and other machine dolls from the same firm. And yet the thing took me aback. To see that curtain go up again and again only to disclose a bewildering profusion of everything that has no business in a play, was an experience for which nothing could quite prepare me. The postal arrangements, the telegraphic arrangements, the police arrangements, the names and addresses, the hours and seasons, the tables of consanguinity, the railway and shipping time-tables, the arrivals and departures, the whole welter of Bradshaw and Baedeker, Court Guide and Post Office Directory whirling round one incredible little stage murder and finally vanishing in a gulp of impossible stage poison, made up an entertainment too Bedlamite for any man with settled wits to preconceive.

The scene [of *Gismonda*] being laid in the Middle Ages, there are no newspapers, letters or telegrams; but this is far from being an advantage, as the characters tell each other the news all through except when a child is dropped into a tiger's cage as a cue for Madame Bernhardt's popular scream.

The Saturday Review, 1 June 1895

Edmond Rostand (1868–1918) is not easy to categorize combining as he did romanticism and realism. *Cyrano de Bergerac* (1897), created by **Constant Coquelin** (1841–1909) who played it over 400 times at the Porte-Saint-Martin, has enjoyed continuing success the world over including film versions.

However, it was in France that the reaction to the (excesses of) the well-made play found its most powerful advocate in the novelist **Émile Zola** (1840–1902). In place of the contrivances, complications and comforting conclusion of the well-made play, Zola, drawing on recent medical research and writing, advocated the exploration of human nature in terms of heredity and environment almost using the stage as a laboratory. Several of his novels were adapted for the theatre by others, but he produced his own stage version of *Thérèse Raquin* (1873), which, together with *Le Naturalisme au Théâtre* (1876–80) provided the rubrics of naturalism for its practitioners.

Naturalism on the stage

The impulse of the century is toward naturalism ... I am waiting for someone to put a man of flesh and bones on the stage, taken from reality, scientifically analysed, and described without one lie ...

I am waiting for environment to determine the characters and the characters to act according to the logic of facts combined with the logic of their own disposition ...

I would ... put him [a man] in his proper surroundings and analyse all the physical and social causes which make him what he is ...

It is up to the dramatic author to make use of environments as novelists do, since the novelists know how to introduce and make such environments real ... Today the naturalistic movement has brought about a more and more perfect exactness in stage scenery.

Émile Zola, *Le Naturalisme au Théâtre*

Antoine and the Théâtre Libre

André Antoine was working as a clerk for the Paris Gas Company when he mounted the Théâtre Libre's first programme of four one-act plays on 30 March 1887. The success of the evening was **Leon Hennique**'s adaptation of *Jacques Damour*, a story by Zola who was present, with Antoine in the title role. Two months later *En Famille*, **Oscar Méténier**'s one-act naturalistic sketch of life in the Paris slums was received with such enthusiasm that Antoine felt able to give up his clerkship to prepare a full season in the autumn. As a means of avoiding censorship and raising capital, the Théâtre Libre was a subscription society and membership swiftly rose from 37 to over 3,000, with early successes including Tolstoy's *The Power of Darkness*, which had been banned in Russia, in February 1888.

Antoine intensified his efforts to achieve the complete illusion of physical reality. True to Zola the setting, the environment which largely determined the lives of the characters, was created with painstaking detail and it was only when this was completed to Antoine's satisfaction that he decided which wall to remove for the audience's benefit. For Fernand Icre's *The Butchers* (1888) he used real carcasses of beef. He introduced Paris audiences to Ibsen (*Ghosts* 1890, *The Wild Duck* 1891) and Strindberg (*Miss Julie* 1893).

The Théâtre Libre toured to Germany, Holland and England and was emulated by Otto Brahm with the Freie Bühne in Berlin from 1889 and J. T. Grein with the Independent Theatre in London from 1891. Though its finances were precarious – bankruptcy in 1897 – the Théâtre Libre achieved great artistic distinction with productions of 184 plays. In 1906 Antoine was appointed sole director of the Odéon, the 1,900 seat theatre in the Latin Quarter, where he further refined stage naturalism.

André Antoine's production of Ibsen's *The Wild Duck*, at the Théâtre Libre, 1891

Anti-realists

Just as naturalism was a reaction against the well-made play, in its turn it produced its own reaction in the so-called anti-realists and symbolists. After the opening of Bayreuth in 1876 Wagner's ideas became better known. Though Adolphe Appia declined Cosima Wagner's invitation to design the costumes at the Festspielhaus in 1888, in *Die Musik und die Inscenierung* (1899) he produced designs showing how the mood and subtext of an opera could be expressed in terms of colour, light and space.

In the meantime, the leading symbolist poet, **Stéphane Mallarmé** (1842–98) was arguing that drama should use the arts of the theatre to evoke the hidden spiritual meaning of life rather than its surface detail. **Aurélien Lugné-Poe** (1869–1940), who had worked with Antoine at the Théâtre Libre, joined forces with **Paul Fort** (1872–1960) at the Théâtre d'Art of which he became director in 1893 renaming it the Théâtre de L'Oeuvre. Of the dramatists (Strindberg, Wilde – *Salomé*) whose work was staged by Lugné-Poe, **Maurice Maeterlinck** (1862–1949) the Belgian poet and dramatist was the leading exponent of symbolism. Following Lugné-Poe's production in 1892, *Pelléas et Mélisande* was performed by Mrs Patrick Campbell and Sarah Bernhardt as well as inspiring Debussy's opera (1902) and *L'Oiseau Bleu/The Blue Bird* (1909) enjoyed international success.

Lugné-Poe's most scandalous production was of **Alfred Jarry**'s (1873–1907) *Ubu Roi* (11 December 1896) which with its foul language, grotesque masks and life-size wicker mannequins offended naturalists and symbolists alike – Antoine rose from his seat in the stalls to express his objections; fights broke out and many left in protest.

Norway

It is ironic that **Henrik Ibsen** (1828–1906) who produced the single most substantial, influential and enduring canon of plays in the nineteenth century, came from a country with very little theatrical tradition. From 1397 to 1814 Norway and Denmark were united with Danish as the official language which, in effect, it continued to be for some time after separation. Although an attempt to establish a Norwegian company had been made in 1825, when the Christiania Theatre (in present-day Oslo), which had opened in 1827, was burnt down in 1835 its replacement was dominated by Danish personnel. It was in Bergen that the fiercely patriotic **Ole Bull**

(1810–80), a celebrated violinist, established the Norwegian Theatre in 1850, which was followed in 1852 by Christiania's Norwegian Theatre.

Ibsen

Ibsen was born in Skien in south-east Norway on 20 March 1828, his early years were blighted by his father's insolvency and at 15 he became an apothecary's assistant in the small coastal town of Grimstad where he remained for six years, fathering an illegitimate child and writing two plays. In 1851 he accepted the post of stage manager at Bull's theatre in Bergen where he spent six years gaining valuable experience in direction, design, management and playwriting; he also travelled to Denmark and Germany to study the theatres there. Although the Bergen theatre had been established to further Norwegian nationalism, the paucity of native drama meant that the repertoire was predominantly foreign with French plays accounting for 75 (21 of them by Scribe) out of the 145 staged whilst Ibsen was there. In 1857 Ibsen became artistic director of the Norwegian Theatre in Christiania, but its finances were precarious and it closed in 1862 after which Ibsen spent two years as literary adviser to the Danish Theatre before leaving for a self-imposed exile which was to last 27 years.

Prior to leaving Norway Ibsen had written nine plays, ranging through romantic comedy, verse drama, tragedy and national history, of which *The Pretenders*, an historical prose tragedy set in thirteenth-century Norway, received a successful production in Christiania in 1864. Nevertheless his next two plays, *Brand* (1866) and *Peer Gynt* (1867), were written to be read rather than staged. After a brief return to Norway in 1874 Ibsen settled in Munich where he wrote *The Pillars of Society*, the first of the great prose dramas with which he made his name. Of these *A Doll's House* (1879) caused an immediate sensation with Norah's slamming of the front door, as she left her apartment and family, echoing far beyond the theatres in which it was performed. *Ghosts* (1881), with its theme of inherited sexual disease and incest, was universally vilified with the conservative critic **Clement Scott** (1841–1904) leading the attack in England.

Clement Scott on *Ghosts*

If people like the discussion of such nasty subjects on the stage, if they care to make the theatre a closed borough and not a free place of assembly, if it is desirable to drive decent-minded women out of the play-house, and to use the auditorium as a hospital-ward or dissecting-room, let it be so. Whatever people desire they will have, and no talking in the world will prevent it. But in our hurry to dramatize the Contagious Diseases Act let us first set about writing a good play.

The Illustrated London News, 21 March 1891

In 1891 Ibsen returned permanently to Norway where, in his last play *When the Dead Awaken* (1899), he developed a more symbolic style. Thus, although Ibsen is principally associated with naturalism, at the beginning and end of his career he wrote plays in other contrasting styles such as verse drama and symbolism.

Bjornstjerne Bjornson (1832–1910)

Bjornson succeeded Ibsen at the Bergen Theatre in 1857. He was a prolific playwright – also a novelist and poet – whose range encompassed historical/patriotic and social/political dramas. The relationship between Bjornson and Ibsen was fraught at times, though their children (Bergliot Bjornson and Sigurd Ibsen) married on 11 October 1892.

Sweden

Despite its earlier tradition of court patronage the Swedish theatre did not produce a dramatist of international stature until **August Strindberg** (1849–1912).

Strindberg

Born in Stockholm, the son of a shipping merchant who went bankrupt, Strindberg trained, but did not qualify, as a doctor. His initial attempt at a theatrical career proving unsuccessful, he worked as a journalist, a librarian and wrote an autobiographical novel (*The Red Room* 1879). Dramaten – the Royal Dramatic Theatre – in Stockholm, where a couple of Strindberg's apprentice pieces were briefly performed in the 1870s, temporarily lost its subsidy in 1888, but in that year *The Father* (1887) was successfully staged at the Freie Bühne in Berlin. In 1889 Strindberg set up his own short-lived Scandinavian Experimental Theatre in Copenhagen (modelled on the Théâtre Libre), where *Miss Julie* (1888), having been banned by the censor, was privately performed. In his preface Strindberg presented his concept of naturalism.

Strindberg's Preface to *Miss Julie*

I have suggested many possible motivations for Miss Julie's unhappy fate. The passionate character of her mother; the upbringing misguidedly inflicted on her by her father; her own character; and the suggestive effect of her fiancé upon her weak and degenerate brain. Also, more immediately the festive atmosphere of Midsummer Night; her father's absence; her menstruation; her association with animals; the intoxicating effect of the dance; the midsummer twilight, the powerfully aphrodisiac influence of the flowers; and, finally, the chance that drove these two people together into a private room – plus of course the passion of the sexually inflamed man [Jean, Miss Julie's father's valet].

This multiplicity of motives is, I like to think, typical of our times.

I have ... confined myself to a simple set, both to enable the characters to accustom themselves to their *milieu*, and to get away from the tradition of scenic luxury. But when one has only one set, one is entitled to demand that it be realistic ... Even if the walls have to be of canvas, it is surely time to stop painting them with shelves and kitchen utensils ... Another perhaps not unnecessary innovation would be the removal of the footlights.

Translated by Michael Meyer

Though he was such a thorough-going practitioner of naturalism in later plays (*The Road to Damascus* 1898–1901, *A Dream Play* 1902 and *Ghost Sonata*, 1907) Strindberg went beneath the exterior to explore the inner, dream, psychological world in what – with hindsight – are regarded as early examples of expressionism.

Expressionism

The exploration of inner states by non-naturalistic means such as powerful colours, intense lighting and exaggerated movement. Linked to the work of artists such as **Edward Munch**.

Russia

During her reign (1762–96) **Empress Catherine the Great**, herself an aspiring dramatist, did much to encourage the theatre. In the early nineteenth century both St Petersburg and Moscow had their Bolshoy (Great) and Maly (Little) theatres which were part of the monopoly enjoyed by the Imperial Theatre Directorate until 1882. In the intervening years a number of talented authors turned their attention to the theatre with lasting benefits.

Dramatists

Alexander Pushkin (1799–1837) who was widely read in European drama, embarked on his nationalistic tragedy *Boris Godunov* (1825) greatly under the influence of Shakespeare. He also wrote a one-act version of the Don Juan legend, *The Stone Guest*, first performed in 1847.

Nikolai Gogol (1809–52), generally regarded as a pioneer realist had the distinction of seeing *The Government Inspector* performed before Tsar Nicholas in St Petersburg on 19 April 1836. Following the Tsar's lead, the audience laughed and applauded Gogol's satire on corrupt bureaucracy, but the ensuing reactionary backlash forced him into a lengthy exile. Although not the originator of the role, **Mikhail Shchepkin** (1788–1863), acclaimed by Stanislavsky as the founder of Russian realistic acting, scored one of his greatest successes as the Mayor, whom he portrayed as a shifty swindler.

Ivan Turgenev (1818–83) the son of wealthy landowners, spent much of his adult life in France and modelled his early one-act comedies on **Alfred de Musset** (1810–57) who, against the prevailing fashion, brought poetry and fantasy back to the theatre. Though it ran into trouble with the censors and was not staged until 1872, *A Month in the Country* (1850) is now regarded as the prototype for Chekhov.

Alexander Ostrovsky (1823–1886), in addition to writing 76 plays, exercised enormous power and influence over the repertoire and direction of the Russian Theatre. *The Thunderstorm*, in which the storm of the title acquires psychological, symbolic and theatrical significance, was first performed at the Moscow Maly Theatre on 16 November 1859.

Leo Tolstoy (1828–1910), the celebrated novelist, wrote six plays of which *The Power of Darkness* (1888), first performed at Antoine's Théâtre Libre having been banned in Russia, depicted the grim conditions of peasant life with merciless realism.

The Moscow Art Theatre

Considerable though the achievements of the nineteenth-century Russian theatre were they do not diminish the significance of the lengthy meeting at the Slavic Bazaar restaurant in Moscow during the summer of 1897 between **Konstantin Stanislavsky** an actor, director and teacher and **Vladimir Nemirovich-Danchenko** (1858–1943) playwright and teacher, who together agreed the principles upon which the Moscow Popular Art Theatre was to be run. The division of duties gave Stanislavsky supremacy 'in matters of stage direction and artistic production' and Nemirovich-Danchenko the 'full power of veto in all questions of literary character', but their shared objectives were: that the needs of the plays and the actors should determine overall policy and organization; that each production should have specially designed settings, properties and costumes; and that performances should be treated as artistic experiences, not social occasions.

In the summer of 1898 the company, which numbered 39, rehearsed at Pushkino, about 48 km (30 miles) from Moscow, for the opening season at their rented home the Hermitage Theatre. The repertoire included Tolstoy's *Tsar Fyodor*, Sophocles' *Antigone*, *The Merchant of Venice*, and Chekhov's *The Seagull*, one play being rehearsed from 11 a.m. to 5 p.m. and another from 7 to 11 p.m. Victor Simov, the talented stage designer in the naturalistic style, was busy making models for the scenery which was being constructed in Moscow.

The season opened on 14 October 1898 with **A.K. Tolstoy's** (1817–75) historical drama *Tsar Fyodor* staged with painstaking attention to its sixteenth-century setting in a manner reminiscent of the Meiningen Company, an association which was reinforced by the productions of Sophocles and Shakespeare. It was not until *The Seagull* on 17 December that the Moscow Art Theatre established its distinctive identity. *The Seagull* had already been performed – disastrously – in 1896 at the Alexandrinsky Theatre in St Petersburg where no-one involved had realized that the play needed a different approach from the rest of the repertoire. This Stanislavsky clearly appreciated.

Stanislavsky on *The Seagull*

Simov understood my plans and purpose of stage direction and began to help me marvellously towards the creation of the mood. On the very fore-stage, right near the footlights, in direct opposition to all the accepted laws and customs of the theatre of that time, almost all the persons in the play sat on a long swinging bench characteristic of Russian country estates, with their backs to the public.

My Life in Art, p.331

Though *The Seagull* achieved no more than moderate success (18 performances in the first season compared with 57 of *Tsar Fyodor*) it invested the Moscow Art Theatre with a sense of identity (it adopted the seagull as its emblem) and encouraged Chekhov to write more plays.

Anton Chekhov (1860–1904)

The son – like Ibsen and Strindberg – of a bankrupt father, Chekhov studied medicine at Moscow University, qualifying in 1884, by which time he had had short stories and humorous sketches published in minor magazines. When he wrote *Ivanov*, his first full-length play, in 1887 he was established as a successful author, though that and his next play *The Wood Demon* (1889) did not add to his reputation. As the owner of the Melikhovo estate, which he bought in 1892, Chekhov was attentive to the welfare, health and education of the peasants living on it, but his own health was failing and a major lung haemorrhage in 1897 brought home to him that he was suffering from advanced consumption. In 1898 he moved to the more sympathetic climate of Yalta which was his base for his few remaining years during which he completed his three masterpieces: *Uncle Vanya* (1899), *Three Sisters* (1901) and *The Cherry Orchard* (1904) all of them produced at the Moscow Art Theatre, the leading lady of which, **Olga Knipper** (1868–1959), he married in 1901.

Beneath an apparently straightforward surface Chekhov created characters of great complexity and, master of naturalism though he was, his plays are suffused with mood and atmosphere and often expand into a symbolic dimension.

Although it was with its naturalistic productions of Chekhov's plays that the Moscow Art Theatre made its reputation, Stanislavsky encouraged other approaches. In 1912 Edward Gordon Craig actually had the opportunity to put his theories into practice with his production of *Hamlet* there. Craig based his design on 'the use of simple convex screens which would be placed on the stage in endless combinations. They hinted at architectural forms, corners, niches, street, alleys, towers, and so on.' (*My Life in Art*, p.471)

Ireland

Craig's movable screens were also used by **W. B. Yeats** (1865–1939) at the Abbey Theatre in Dublin in 1911. Though the Abbey, which had been founded in 1904 by Yeats, **Lady Gregory** (1852–1932) and the Fay brothers with the financial assistance of **Annie Horniman** (1860–1937), is closely associated with the naturalism – rural – of **J. M. Synge** (1871–1909) and – urban – of **Sean O'Casey** (1880–1964) its original goal was to encourage poetic drama on the grand scale about Irish history and legend. For his own plays Yeats required only a bare stage with a few emblematic properties which together with music, dance and masks would allow the verse to shine through, achieving a quasi-ritual effect. Some of Yeats's later plays were influenced by the stylized *Nō* drama of Japan.

Through a combination of independent development and cross-fertilization, during the nineteenth century the theatres of Europe had progressed on parallel lines, developing from verse drama – often on nationalistic themes – to naturalism and beyond that to symbolism and/or expressionism. Plays by Ibsen, Strindberg and Chekhov have become and are likely to remain central to the theatrical repertoire the world over.

9 | ALL THE WORLD'S A STAGE

Many of the major movements of the twentieth-century theatre can be traced back to the nineteenth century, but they did not necessarily achieve their full realization in their country of origin. Political events – two World Wars, the Russian revolution – and technological changes, both within and outside (film, television, video) the theatre, have been significant factors in the twentieth century.

The Repertory Movement

In Britain the late nineteenth-century theatre was dominated by the actor-manager and touring. In November 1901 the *Era* listed 143 touring companies on the road or, more accurately, on the railway, which on Sundays became the lifeline by which actors (their scenery and costumes) were transported to their next booking, sometimes at the opposite end of the country. There was a clear distinction between number one dates in the major cities, in which the real stars performed, and the number two and number three bookings, and the fortunes of companies and individual actors could be charted according to their – changing – position. The system was not without its merits: it brought provincial audiences a constantly changing diet, albeit one of varying quality over which as consumers they could exercise little control; for the actors, though it meant an itinerant life, a role once learnt could keep them in work for a year or more; for the touring managers it provided a good return on investment and for the theatre managers minimal risk. What it failed to do was to enable a community to develop its own taste and a theatre company its own artistic policy and style.

The national, court and state theatres of Europe provided models as Matthew Arnold pointed out when the Comédie-Française visited London in 1879.

The French Play in London

But I see our community turning to the theatre with eagerness and
finding the English theatre without organization, or purpose, or
dignity, and no modern English drama at all except a fantastical one.
And then I see the French company from the chief theatre in Paris
showing themselves to us in London – a society of actors admirable
in organization, purpose, and dignity, with a modern drama ...

Give them [a company of good actors] a theatre at the West End. Let
them have a grant from your Science and Art Department ... Try
them. When your institution in the West End of London has become
a success, plant a second of like kind in the East. The people *will*
have the theatre; then make it a good one. Let your two or three
provincial towns institute, with municipal subsidy and co-operation,
theatres such as you institute in the metropolis with state subsidy and
co-operation. So you will restore the English theatre.

The Nineteenth Century, 6 August 1879

As already noted, some private initiatives did take place in London. J. T.
Grein's Independent Theatre (modelled on Antoine's Théâtre Libre) in
1891; the Stage Society in 1899; and the Vedrenne-Barker management at
the Royal Court 1904. William Archer and Granville Barker published *A
National Theatre: Scheme and Estimates* (1907), but it fell on deaf ears. In
1910 **Charles Frohman** (1860–1915), the youngest of three American
brothers, all theatre managers, launched a full-scale repertory programme
at the Duke of York's Theatre featuring **Granville Barker**'s *The Madras
House*, one-act plays by **J. M. Barrie**, (1860–1937), **John Galsworthy**'s
(1867–1933) *Justice* and **Shaw**'s *Misalliance*. Without subsidy the venture
was doomed, but it demonstrated how a genuine repertoire system
(performances of four different plays in a week) worked and with *Justice*
(a protest against the penal system of the day) it premiered a play which
was not only to feature in many provincial repertories but also to serve as
a model for aspiring repertory authors.

Manchester

It was in Manchester, the scene of Charles Calvert's great Shakespearean
revivals a tradition maintained there and elsewhere by his son **Louis
Calvert** (1859–1923), that the first repertory theatre was established at the

Gaiety Theatre in 1908, following an encouraging trial season at the Midland Hotel the previous year. The Glasgow Repertory Company followed in 1909, Liverpool in 1911, Birmingham in 1913. As George Rowell and Anthony Jackson have observed: 'Broadly repertory theatres in Britain have seen themselves as determinedly non-commercial in approach, based in and serving a specific community or region and providing a wide range of plays, new and classic, challenging and popular.' (*The Repertory Movement*, 1984, p.2) In its early days the repertory movement was closely associated with naturalism, especially in Manchester where the so-called Manchester School produced realistic dramas of provincial life: **Stanley Houghton** (1881–1913) *Hindle Wakes* (1912) and **Harold Brighouse** (1882–1958) *Hobson's Choice* (1916).

Tea and milk

It has been said that the English Repertory Movement was founded on tea and milk since it was in those two commodities that the families of Miss Horniman (Manchester) and Barry Jackson (Birmingham) made their fortunes.

Annie Horniman (1860–1937) sponsored the production of Shaw's *Arms and the Man* at the Avenue Theatre in 1894. She worked for five years as W. B. Yeats's private secretary and in 1904 financed the founding of the Abbey Theatre, Dublin to the tune of £13,000. Following successive disagreements she finally withdrew her support in 1910, by which time she had already set up the Gaiety which she supported until 1921.

Barry Jackson (1879–1961), uniquely, had a purpose-built theatre designed for his repertory company. From 1913 to 1935 Jackson underwrote the costs of the Birmingham Repertory Theatre. Between 1929 and 1937 he also ran the Malvern Theatre Festival and was director of the Shakespeare Memorial Theatre from 1945 to 1948. Jackson was knighted in 1925.

American theatre

Although some Americans individually helped to narrow the divide between their theatre and Europe's, the American stage was slow both to develop its own identity and to adopt the innovations of the European *avant-garde*. **Edwin Booth** (1833–93) and **Mary Anderson** (1859–1940) pursued their acting careers on both sides of the Atlantic; **Augustin Daly** (1838–99) managed – and owned – theatres in London and New York; **David Belasco**'s (1853–1931) prodigious activities as playwright, director and manager were on a truly international scale, and **Winthrop Ames** (1871–1937) and his millionaire patrons consciously modelled the ill-fated New Theatre, New York (1909) on National Theatres in Europe. However, it was upon more modest foundations that the twentieth-century American theatre rose.

Little Theatres

In 1901 the amateur Hull-House Players set up in Chicago to stage quality plays, which they believed could have 'a salutary influence on the community'. The movement really took off following the visit by the Abbey Theatre, whose origins were amateur, to the United States in 1911. There was a parallel Little Theatre movement in England, notably the Maddermarket Theatre in Norwich, but, increasingly the need was being met by repertory theatres, though sometimes, as in Sheffield, these developed from a Little Theatre.

The Provincetown Players

In 1915 a group of amateurs from Iowa led by **George Cram Cook** (1873–1924) gave some performances of short plays, which they had written themselves, beneath the porch of a building in the small coastal resort of Provincetown, Massachusetts. The next year the Provincetown Players staged *Bound East for Cardiff* by Eugene O'Neill with such success that in November they transferred to New York (Greenwich Village) where they continued until 1929.

Eugene O'Neill (1888–1953)

The son of popular romantic/melodramatic actor **James O'Neill** (1847–1920), who together with other members of his family provided the prototypes for his *Long Day's Journey Into Night* (1939–41), Eugene O'Neill abandoned his studies at Princeton University in favour of (amongst other things) mining and beachcombing, though he later attended **George Pierce Baker**'s (1866–1935) prestigious playwriting course at Harvard. O'Neill's output of over 50 plays ranged from one-act (*Fog* 1914) to plays of Wagnerian length (*Strange Interlude* 1928), his models from Sophocles to Shakespeare, from Ibsen – through Strindberg – to the Czech expressionist **Karel Capek** (1890–1938). O'Neill combined prose realism and expressionist invention, but of the two it was the former that he used to lasting effect in his masterpieces *The Iceman Cometh* (1939) and the aforementioned *Long Day's Journey Into Night*.

Susan Glaspell (1876–1948)

Susan Glaspell, who was married to George Cram Cook, was the other major talent to emerge from Provincetown. She used realism (*Trifles* 1916), symbolism and expressionism (*The Verge* 1921) to explore the inner lives of her characters, the overwhelming majority of which were female.

Between the World Wars

The inter-war years were exciting for the American stage. The commercial theatre's stronghold was Broadway with **Moss Hart** (1904–61) and **George Kaufman** (1889–1961) providing hits like *You Can't Take It With You* (1936), the **Gershwins, George** (1898–1937) and **Ira** (1896–1983) produced a string of successful musicals (*Lady be Good* 1924) though their American folk opera *Porgy and Bess*, now regarded as their finest achievement, was not well received by press or public in 1935 when it was produced by the Theatre Guild. The Theatre Guild, which had evolved in 1919 from the Washington Square Players (1915), specialized in modern European plays – Shaw and expressionist works such as **Georg Kaiser**'s (1878–1945) and new American drama, notably by **Elmer Rice** (1892–1967; *The Adding Machine* 1923), **Robert C. Sherwood** (1896–1955; *Reunion in Vienna* 1931), **Maxwell Anderson** (1888–1959; *Elizabeth of England* 1930) and O'Neill.

Key figures were **Lee Simonson** (1888–1967) the scene designer and **Lee Strasberg** (1901–82), who was in the separatist group which in 1931 left the Theatre Guild to form the Group Theatre, modelled on the Moscow Art Theatre. Strasberg and **Harold Clurman** (1901–80) assembled a group of actors who worked intensively together through improvisation and other exercises to create the depth of psychological characterization about which Stanislavsky had written in *An Actor Prepares* (1926). Strasberg continued his work at the Actors' Studio, numbering Marlon Brando, James Dean and Marilyn Monroe amongst the practitioners of, so-called, Method acting.

The Group Theatre's record on new plays was not especially strong with the exception of **Clifford Odets** (1906–63) the most politically extreme dramatist of the period, who voiced the dissatisfactions of the under-privileged in plays such as *Waiting for Lefty* (1935). In that year the Federal Theatre Project, the first government-financed theatre in the USA, was established under the Works Progress Administration giving employment to many (10,000 at one time) and entertainment to even more (12 million in New York alone).

Events in Europe conspired to bring the German dramatist **Bertolt Brecht** (1898–1956) to Hollywood in 1941, but before he returned to Berlin in 1948 he had come under the scrutiny of the Congressional Un-American Activities committee, as later did Arthur Miller.

Arthur Miller (1915–) and Tennessee Williams (1911–83)

Miller, the heterosexual (Marilyn Monroe was his second wife) Jew from New York and Williams, the homosexual Southerner from Mississippi quickly established themselves as the twin pillars of post-war American theatre, the former with *All My Sons* (1947), *Death of a Salesman* (1949) and *The Crucible* (1953) and the latter with *A Street Car Named Desire* (1947). In neither case has their later work matched their early achievements. Of the two, Miller impresses as the cerebral craftsman, Williams as the intuitive artist.

Edward Albee (1928–), an allusive and elusive stylist; **Neil Simon** (1927–), a popular dramatist capable of wit and subtlety; and **David Mamet** (1947–), master of the minimal plot and the menace of language, have all achieved international status.

France

Although Zola and Antoine had made significant contributions to the *avant-garde,* the French theatre as a whole continued to be dominated by adulterous farces and spectacle which so incensed **Jacques Copeau** (1879–1949) that in 1913 he opened the Théâtre du Vieux – Colombier on the left bank of the Seine and dedicated it principally to the classics, especially Shakespeare and Molière. In his pursuit of *le Beau, le Bien et le Vrai* (the beautiful, the good and the true) Copeau set exacting standards for his company for which **Louis Jouvet** (1887–1951) designed a simple, ascetic, quasi-Elizabethan stage.

Copeau exercised far-reaching influence through numerous disciples. Louis Jouvet formed a close collaborative relationship with the dramatist **Jean Giraudoux** (1882–1944) and later directed work by **Jean-Paul Sartre** (1905–80) and **Jean Genet** (1910–86). In 1927 Jouvet was co-founder of the Cartel, a group of companies committed to mutual support of each other's work in the face of what they regarded as the trivializing of it by critics. The other members of the Cartel were **Charles Dullin** (1885–1949) who had been an actor with Copeau, director **Gaston Baty** (1885–1952) and the Russian emigré **Georges Pitoëff** (1884–1939) whose Paris production of Pirandello's *Six Characters in Search of an Author* (1921) caused a sensation.

Luigi Pirandello (1867–1936) the son of a well-to-do Sicilian family, established himself as a novelist, poet and academic before turning to playwriting following the collapse of the family business (sulphur mines) and his wife's mental illness. The themes which he explored in plays such as *Six Characters in Search of an Author*, *Naked* (1922) and *Henry IV* (1922) have proved to be seminal in the twentieth-century theatre: sanity/madness, art/life, metadrama and (non-) communication.

In 1929 Copeau's own nephew **Michel Saint-Denis** (1897–1971) set up La Campagnie des Quinze which toured extensively, including in England, where Saint-Denis remained in 1935, producing Gielgud in **Andre Obey**'s (1892–1975) *Noah* and, together with Peggy Ashcroft and Michael Redgrave, in his fabled *Three Sisters* (1938).

Antonin Artaud (1896–1948) gained experience with Dullin, Lugné-Poe and Pitoëff before establishing the Théâtre Alfred Jarry with writers Robert Aran and **Roger Vitrac** (1899–1952) in 1926. It was not until 1935 that he had the means for his long-planned Theatre of Cruelty, but even then he had to abandon his scenario *The Conquest of Mexico* for his more modest adaptation of P. B. Shelley's verse tragedy *The Cenci* – staged on 6 May 1935 at the Folies-Wagram. Though *The Cenci* was both an artistic and financial failure which effectively ended Artaud's theatrical career, his writings have been highly influential, expecially *The Theatre and its Double* (1938) in which he argued that the theatre should rediscover a sense of danger in which words would be only one element harnessed with space, movement and so on to create 'total theatre'. His concept of the 'single creator', in place of the duality between author and producer, has been most nearly achieved by **Jean-Louis Barrault** (1910–94) and **Peter Brook** (1925–).

Russia

Vsevolod Meyerhold (1874–1940), of German parentage, studied under Nemirovich-Danchenko at the drama school of the Moscow Philharmonic Society and appeared in the Moscow Art Theatre's first season. An admirer of Gogol and the Symbolists, Meyerhold was both politically and artistically radical which did not endear him to the theatre-goers of Kherson in the Ukraine when he ran two seasons (1902–4) at the municipal theatre. He fared little better when he relocated to Tiflis (Tbilisi), the capital of Georgia, but in 1905 Stanislavsky, ever encouraging of genuine talent, invited Meyerhold to run the new studio theatre at the Moscow Art Theatre. There Meyerhold experimented with stylization in which the actors' vocal delivery and movement were co-ordinated with the music, costumes and set to produce an anti-illusionistic effect totally at odds with naturalism.

In 1906 Meyerhold was invited by the actress **Vera Komisarjevskaya** (1864–1910) to become artistic director of her theatre in St Petersburg. By then Meyerhold had read Georg Fuch's *The Stage of the Future* the anti-realistic principles of which he put into effect in his production of *Hedda Gabler* (10 November 1906) in which the acting area was confined to a strip, 10 m (33 feet) wide by 3.7 m (12 feet) deep, at the front of the stage and the scenery (a simple backdrop) and costumes (suggestive of character rather than true to a period) were determinedly symbolic. In 1908 Mme Komisarjevskaya dispensed with Meyerhold's services appointing her half-brother **Fedor (Theodore) Komisarjevsky** (1882–1954), who after the revolution worked extensively in Britain, in his place.

Between 1908 and 1918 Meyerhold ran the Imperial theatres in St Petersburg, but after the October Revolution he swiftly identified himself with the Bolsheviks and joined the (Communist) party. In November 1918 Meyerhold and the playwright **Vladimir Mayakovsky** (1893–1930) marked the first anniversary of the revolution with *Mystery-Bouffee* their satirical fantasy about creating paradise on earth and in 1920 Meyerhold was duly appointed Head of the Theatre Division of the People's Commissariat for Education, but he resigned after only a few months.

Though the Soviet regime notionally encouraged theatres – Moscow, which had 16 in 1917, had 60 in 1934 – following Lenin's New Economic Policy of 1921 it imposed strict controls which were greatly strengthened by Stalin whose censors (Glavrepertkom) turned down half the plays planned for the 1936/7 season. Meyerhold and other directors (**Alexander Tairov** 1885–1950 and **Evgeny Vakhtangov** 1883–1923) who had pioneered innovative movements from symbolism to constructionism were exhorted to practise the propaganda of social realism. Accused of formalism, Meyerhold defended his ideals, was arrested and, if not executed, died in a labour camp.

Germany

Max Reinhardt (1873–1943)

Born near Vienna Reinhardt (originally Goldmann) adopted his name when he began his theatrical career – against his family's wishes – at the age of 18. Whilst acting in Salzburg he so impressed Otto Brahm, who was then running the Deutsches Theater in Berlin, that he received an engagement there – in 1894 – and remained for eight years. In 1903 he was free to develop his own ideas at the Kleines (Little Theatre) where he sought to replace the dourness so often associated with naturalism with gaiety and colour, despite which he and his partner Richard Vallentin staged Gorky's *The Lower Depths* with such success that they took on the much larger Neues Theater am Schiffbauerdamm as well. There Reinhardt experimented with lighting and installed a revolving stage which he put to spectacular effect in his 1905 revival of *A Midsummer Night's Dream*, a play to which he was to return many times (OUDS 1933, Warner Bros film 1935) always recreating it in a manner appropriate to the circumstances. Versatile and eclectic though Reinhardt was, he consistently held ideas about the actor ('It is to the actor and to no one else that the theatre belongs') and the power of illusion in the theatre.

Reinhardt's creativity was matched by his energy. From 1905 to 1920 he ran two Berlin theatres (the Kammerspiele/Chamber and the Deutsches Theater), personally directing 123 productions with many overseas in addition. Of these, *Oedipus Rex* which toured Europe after opening in Munich in 1910, and *The Miracle*, which was premiered before an audience of 30,000 at the Olympic Exhibition Hall, London, 1911, were the most spectacular. In 1920 Reinhardt launched the Salzburg festival with *Jedermann*, **Hugo von Hofmannsthal**'s (1874–1929) version of the morality play, and thereafter spent more of his time in Austria before taking up residence in the United States in 1933 – a refugee from the Nazis.

Erwin Piscator (1893–1966)

His experience as a conscript during the First World War politicized Piscator who became a Marxist and member of the German Communist Party. Piscator combined radicalism, populism and propaganda. Thus his technical innovations, such as the use of film, were intended to make his work more accessible to the people. His outstanding successes at the Volksbühne Theater were **Ernst Toller**'s (1893–1939) *Hurrah, We Live* (1927) and **Jaroslav Hašek**'s novel *The Good Soldier Schwejk* (1928) adapted for the stage in 25 scenes by Piscator, **Felix Gasbarra** and **Bertolt Brecht** many of whose techniques as a dramatist and director were derived from Piscator.

Like Brecht, Piscator took refuge from Hitler in the United States and like him returned to Germany, where he took over the Freie Volksbühne in 1962 his repertoire including new plays by **Rolf Hochhuth** (1931–) and **Peter Weiss** (1916–82).

To England

The employment prospects for a director forced into exile by repressive totalitarianism (Soviet or Nazi) were obviously better than for an actor for whom language differences constituted an insuperable barrier. Nevertheless, amongst the many adjustments directors such as Reinhardt and Komisarjevsky had to make when pursuing their careers in England must have been the realization that the function which they fulfilled in the theatre was still at an early stage of development.

Though Irving had been as consummate a director as any of his contemporaries within or beyond Britain his genius as an actor tended to eclipse his other skills. Furthermore by his example the actor-manager had become the apex of the profession to which new generations (**Donald Wolfit** 1902–68) still aspired. The situation was intensified by the absence of state subsidized theatres with their hierarchy of artistic, administrative, literary and coaching positions. The nearest England got to the continental idea of a state theatre was the Old Vic in London and the Shakespeare Memorial Theatre in Stratford-upon-Avon.

The Old Vic

Unfashionably located south of the River Thames the Coburg, as it was originally known, opened in 1818. By the time Charles Kingsley wrote *Alton Locke* (1851) it was frequented by a disorderly rabble who took as much pleasure in the consumption of alcohol as in the dramatic fare on the stage. On Boxing Day 1880 it was re-opened by Emma Cons as the Royal Victoria Coffee Hall dedicated to providing the habitués of music-hall and such like diversions 'an entertainment which shall amuse without degrading them, and to which men may take their wives and children without shaming or harming them'. In October 1881 William Poel was appointed as manager presiding over a programme which endeavoured to balance the attractions of entertainment with the benefits of education.

William Poel (1852–1934)

Though he worked as an actor and manager, Poel's driving passion was the production of Elizabethan plays on 'authentic' stages performed in 'period' style. In 1881 he staged the bad quarto of *Hamlet* at the St George's Hall on a bare stage with himself as the Prince. His 1893 production of, the then little-known, *Measure for Measure* was more successful and in 1894 Poel founded the Elizabethan Stage Society over which he presided until its demise in 1905. During that time many plays by Shakespeare and his contemporaries were staged as was the medieval morality play *Everyman* (1901) the popularity of which was furthered on both sides of the Atlantic by **Philip Ben Greet** (1857–1936). Poel's widespread influence extended to **Ben Iden Payne** (1881–1976), who in 1908 launched Miss Horniman's Gaiety Theatre with a production of *Measure for Measure* in the Poel style. **Edith Evans** (1888–1976) began her career with Poel and in 1921 **Nugent Monck** (1877–1958) created a small-scale Elizabethan theatre, the Maddermarket, for the amateur Norwich Players. However, it was by Harley Granville Barker that Poel's ideas were most imaginatively developed.

Harley Granville Barker (1877–1946)

By the time he turned to Shakespeare Barker had already established his reputation as an actor, director, manager and dramatist, but his Savoy Theatre productions of *The Winter's Tale*, *Twelfth Night* (both 1912) and *A Midsummer Night's Dream* (1914) constituted a watershed in

Shakespearean production. No antiquarian, Barker put the Elizabethan principles of an ensemble company of actors, minimal scenery on a stage to which an apron had been added, fluent verse-speaking and a full text into effect in a refreshingly contemporary manner. Thereafter, Barker forsook the professional theatre and devoted himself to writing, including his *Prefaces to Shakespeare* 1927–46.

Twelfth Night at the Savoy Theatre

Thus, indeed, Shakespeare lives again, by virtue of scholarship and taste, a quick sympathetic fancy, above all by the resolve to let him be spoken as he wrote, and be played as in the main he and his fellow-actors chose to play. All is over at the Savoy in three hours in a representation broken only by two brief intervals, and I do not believe that three hours of such unmeasured enjoyment are to be spent in any theatre in London.

The Nation, 23 November 1912

The attraction of Shakespeare to **Lilian Baylis** (1874–1937), who took over the Old Vic from her aunt Emma Cons in 1912, was a mixture of patriotism and patronage as Ben Greet's schools matinees attracted large attendances during the First World War. Ingenuity triumphed over difficult circumstances with actresses – **Sybil Thorndike** (1882–1976) as Prince Hal – being cast in male roles. Without subsidy, committed to cheap seats and with only occasional donations from well-wishers, Lilian Baylis continued to run the Old Vic on the proverbial shoe-string for years to come, much to the frustration of Tyrone Guthrie. In 1931 Lilian Baylis opened the rebuilt Sadler's Wells Theatre as the home of ballet and opera, appointing Ninette de Valois as ballet-mistress.

Tyrone Guthrie (1900–71)

Following repertory with **J. B. Fagan** (1873–1933) at the Oxford Playhouse and with **Terence Gray** (1895–1987) at the Festival Theatre, Cambridge, Guthrie's work for the Old Vic spanned the years from 1933 to 1945. Eclectic in approach, his successes included two *Hamlets*, one in modern dress with **Alec Guinness** (1914–) in 1938, the other – more conventional – in 1937 with **Laurence Olivier** (1907–89) being seen at Elsinore. After the war Guthrie took a leading role in setting up the Edinburgh Festival and consolidated his position as an international director, especially in Stratford, Ontario and Minneapolis at both of which theatres with thrust stages were built which became models for Chichester and Sheffield amongst others. Guthrie was knighted in 1961.

Stratford-upon-Avon

The Shakespeare Memorial Theatre, Stratford-upon-Avon, 1932

With the patronage and support of successive generations of the Flower family the 1879 Shakespeare Memorial Theatre hosted annual seasons until it was burnt down in March 1926. From 1919 **William Bridges-Adams** (1889–1965), who had worked with Poel, had been the director as he continued to be until 1934, presiding over the building of the replacement 1932 Memorial Theatre, designed by Elizabeth Scott. The time was not propitious for theatre design and Scott's theatre with its stage and auditorium divided by a structurally immovable – too narrow, too low

– proscenium arch showed a greater debt to cinema design than to the growing awareness of the Elizabethan relationship between actors and their audience. Many shared the reaction of Sir Edward Elgar – 'so unspeakably ugly and wrong'. Some of the most effective productions in the new theatre were those by **Theodore Komisarjevsky** who, designing his own sets, costumes and lighting, applied formalized techniques, unburdened by the accretions of English traditions.

Dramatists

The first four decades of the twentieth century had not proved to be fertile ground for new dramatists. Of the major talents to emerge at the end of the previous century Shaw went on to complete his masterpieces *Pygmalion* (1914) and *St Joan* (1923), but it was **T. S. Eliot** (1888–1965) who showed greater dramatic originality in *Murder in the Cathedral* (1935). **Somerset Maugham** (1874–1965) honed the well-made play and **J. B. Priestley** (1894–1984) dramatized the time theories currently in vogue, but it was **Noel Coward** who swiftly established himself an international reputation.

Noel Coward (1899–1973)

At the age of 11 Coward impressed (not altogether favourably) the distinguished comic actor **Charles Hawtrey** from whom he learnt the skills which he was to deploy not only as an actor but also as a dramatist. *The Vortex*, with its themes of drugs and incest, made Coward an *enfant terrible* when it was first performed in 1924 with the author as Nicky Lancaster. *Hay Fever* provided less contentious fare in 1925 with **Marie Tempest** (1864–1942) as Judith Bliss. By the outbreak of war Coward had added his classic comedies *Private Lives* 1930, *Design for Living* 1932 and *Present Laughter* 1939 to his credits as a playwright and actor, alongside his achievements as a lyricist and composer (*Words and Music* 1932, *Operette* 1937). During the course of the Second World War Coward answered the call of patriotism with the films *In Which We Serve* (1942), which he produced and David Lean directed, and *This Happy Breed* (1943). *Blithe Spirit*, which had been a stage success (1941) was filmed in 1944, the year in which Coward wrote the screenplay for *Brief Encounter*, with which David Lean created his masterpiece of film realism. The post-war climate, especially after 1956, was unsympathetic to Coward, who worked extensively in cabaret, but he returned to form as dramatist – and actor – with *Suite in Three Keys* 1966, having derived enormous satisfaction from the early inclusion of *Hay Fever* in the National Theatre's repertoire (1964). 'The Master', as he was known, was knighted in 1970.

The Second World War

In contrast to the First World War, when the musical *Chu Chin Chow* ran for 2,238 performances, the government recognized early in the Second World War that culture would be an important means of raising the nation's spirits and as such should receive government funding. In January 1940 the Council for the Encouragement of Music and the Arts (CEMA) was set up with a Treasury grant and support from the Pilgrim Trust (until 1942). Its remit was to provide concerts and plays for people who might not normally attend them in places where they might not expect to find them (concerts at the National Gallery; the Old Vic touring to mining towns).

The Arts Council

Thanks largely to the economist **John Maynard (Lord) Keynes** (1883–1946), who had married the ballerina Lydia Lopokova in 1925 and financed the Arts Theatre Cambridge (1935), the work of CEMA, of which he had been chairman, was perpetuated in peacetime with the formation of the Arts Council of Great Britain (August 1946). The Arts Council's purpose – 'to develop a greater knowledge, understanding and practice of the Fine Arts, to increase their accessibility to the public and to improve their standard of execution' – was never going to be easily achieved and it has always been assailed by critics who either disapprove of it in principle or regard it as ineffective.

Harlequinade

JACK: Social purpose, Mr Burton.

BURTON: Social purpose? Now what the blazes is that when it's at home.

JACK: As far as I can see it means playing Shakespeare to audiences who'd rather go to the films; while audiences who'd rather go to Shakespeare are driven to the films because they haven't got Shakespeare to go to – it's all got something to do with the new Britain and apparently it's an absolutely splendid idea.

Terence Rattigan, 1948

Terence Rattigan (1911–77)

Rattigan, who dominated the post-war theatre with well-crafted pieces such as *The Winslow Boy* (1946), *The Browning Version* (1948) and *Separate Tables* (1954) which were generally produced in the West End by the prestigious H. M. Tennent management, created the character of Aunt Edna as the embodiment of the middle-brow theatre-goer. In his review of *Separate Tables* **Kenneth Tynan** (1927–80) confronted Aunt Edna with a Young Perfectionist who concluded his account of Rattigan's double-bill with an invitation.

YP: Will you accompany me on a second visit tomorrow?

AE: With great pleasure. Clearly, there is something here for both of us.

YP: Yes. But not quite enough for either of us.

Imports

During the 1950s, Kenneth Tynan, first in the (London) *Evening Standard*, then in the *Observer* surveyed the London theatre, the highlights of which were usually foreign imports: from American musicals (*Guys and Dolls* 1952, *West Side Story* 1958) and drama (Miller's *The Crucible* 1954 and Williams' *Cat on a Hot Tin Roof* 1958); from France, **Samuel Beckett**'s (1906–89) *Waiting for Godot*, directed by **Peter Hall** (1930–) **Giraudoux** (1882–1944); **Ionesco** (1909–94) brandleader of the Theatre of the Absurd; **Jean Genet** (1910–86) in the footsteps of Artaud and the more mainstream **Jean Anouilh** (1910–87), for whom **Christopher Fry** (1907–) a verse dramatist in his own right, was an eloquent translator.

Then in May 1956 Brecht's Berliner Ensemble came to London's Palace Theatre in *The Caucasian Chalk Circle*, *Mother Courage* and *Trumpets and Drums*. There had been some English Brecht productions: **Joan Littlewood** (1914–) 'over-parted and underhearted' as Mother Courage (1955) and **Peggy Ashcroft** (1907–91) inappropriately suggestive of 'Aladdin as it might be sketched by Princess Badroulbadour', but in comparison the Berliner Ensemble were a revelation. Tynan was rhapsodic, extolling the set and props – 'against a high, encircling, off-white backcloth we see nothing but solid, selected objects', 'the famous "alienation effect"', the 'magnificent songs' and costumes which looked 'as if people and not puppets had worn them'.

Tynan at the Berliner Ensemble in London

It is possible to enter the Palace Theatre wearing the familiar British smile of so-unsophisticated-my-dear-and-after-all-we've rather-*had*-Expressionism (what do such people think Expressionism was?) and it is possible to leave with the same faint smile intact. It is possible: but not pleasant to contemplate.

Tynan was, of course, already a convert having seen the Berliner Ensemble in Berlin and Paris, but in him Brecht had an advocate whose influence was to spread beyond the columns of newspapers to the stage of the National Theatre of which Tynan became literary manager on its foundation in 1963.

Bertolt Brecht (1898–1956)

During his early career in Berlin Brecht came under the influence of Reinhardt and Piscator, from the latter of whom he developed many of the multi-media techniques which were to be a hall-mark of his work. Many of Brecht's early plays were adaptations of English originals: *Edward II* from Marlowe (1924) and *The Threepenny Opera* (1928), a reworking of Gay's *The Beggar's Opera* with music by **Kurt Weill** (1900–50). Forced to leave Germany together with his second wife actress **Helene Weigel** (1900–71) in 1933, Brecht spent his extended exile first in Scandinavia and then (from 1941) in the United States. Thus his major plays *Mother Courage* (1939), *The Good Person of Setzuan* (1940), *The Caucasian Chalk Circle* (1945) and *Galileo* revised for **Charles Laughton** (1899–1962) were not written in his native land. Having taken certain precautions – an Austrian passport, a Swiss bank account and a West German publisher – in 1948 Brecht returned to Berlin where the Communist East German government placed the Theater am Schiffbauerdamm at his disposal together with the resources to run it. There has been a great deal of speculation about Brecht's politics. Marxist though he was, it is unclear whether he actually joined the Communist Party. With the collapse of communism in the late 1980s propaganda on its behalf hardly provides the best foundation for survival in the theatrical repertoire; but Brecht's best plays are made of more durable material, whether or not they are produced in accordance with his own model-books.

Brecht's distinction between the Dramatic and Epic forms of theatre is now generally accepted and, despite problems in translation, his concept of *Verfremdungseffekt*/alienation effect, by which he seems to have meant recurrent changes in perception (by both characters and audience) created by shocks and surprises designed to prevent uncritical identification, has acquired aficionados the world over.

The English Stage Company

Appropriately it was at the Royal Court Theatre, home to the pioneering Vedrenne-Barker season of 1904, that the post-war renaissance of English drama took place. Established in 1956 with **George Devine** (1910–65) as its artistic director the English Stage Society was inaugurated with novelist Angus Wilson's *The Mulberry Bush* (2 April 1956), which had already been staged without much success at the Bristol Old Vic; it received mixed reviews. This was followed by Miller's *The Crucible* which had also been seen previously in Bristol (1954). Both plays achieved a respectable 45 per cent of capacity, but the tide turned decisively on 8 May with *Look Back in Anger* by a young repertory theatre actor **John Osborne** (1929–94). Not everyone shared Tynan's enthusiasm, but he undoubtedly caught the mood when he ended his review: 'I doubt if I could love anyone who did not wish to see *Look Back in Anger*. It is the best young play of its decade.' Though Jimmy Porter was dubbed the original 'angry young man', structurally *Look Back in Anger* is a conventional three-act piece of naturalism, but in *The Entertainer* (1957) with Laurence Olivier and *Luther* (1961) with **Albert Finney** (1936–) Osborne experimented with a freer, more episodic form.

Encouraged by Osborne's success, a generation of Court (or 'Kitchen sink') dramatists sprang up including **John Arden** (1930–), **Arnold Wesker** (1932–), **N. F. Simpson**, (1919–) **Willis Hall** (1929–) and **Ann Jellicoe** (1927–) whose work shared the repertoire with continental plays and some English classics.

The Royal Court had no monopoly on the sudden surge of new writing and at the Theatre Royal, Stratford East, Joan Littlewood staged **Brendan Behan**'s (1923–64) *The Quare Fellow* (1956) followed by *The Hostage* (1958) and 21-year-old **Shelagh Delaney**'s (1939–) *A Taste of Honey* (1958) which transferred to the West End as did Theatre Workshop's satirical documentary of the First World War, *Oh What a Lovely War* (1963).

Neither the Royal Court nor Theatre Workshop could claim credit for discovering the dramatist who by common consent was the greatest to emerge in the 1950s: Harold Pinter.

Harold Pinter (1930–)

Born in Hackney of Jewish parents, Pinter attended the Royal Academy of Dramatic Art and worked as an actor in repertory, with Anew McMaster in Ireland and Donald Wolfit. His first (one-act) play *The Room* was staged by the Drama Department of the University of Bristol in 1957 and his first full-length play *The Birthday Party* arrived at the Lyric Theatre, Hammersmith on 19 May 1958 after a short provincial tour. The receipts, which for the first night were a respectable £140, slumped to £16 on the second and a mere £2-9s (£2.45) for the Thursday matinee. **Harold Hobson's** (1891–1973) enthusiastic review in *The Sunday Times* came too late to rescue *The Birthday Party* which had been taken off on the preceding night. Hobson identified Pinter's strengths as his ability to entertain, mystify and terrorize his audience and hailed him as 'the most original, disturbing and arresting talent in theatrical London'. Such a talent was bound to assert itself and during the 1960s and 1970s Pinter achieved critical and public acclaim with *The Caretaker* (1960), *The Homecoming* (1965), *Old Times* (1971) and *No Man's Land* (1974). In addition to which he wrote film scripts and directed plays by other dramatists (notably **Simon Gray** 1936–) as he still continues to do alongside the resumption of his acting career. At its best the surface simplicity of Pinter's dialogue – interspersed with the famous pauses – conveys the ambiguous complexity and emotional power of his characters with intrinsic theatrical flair.

The regions

Though English local authorities were slow to take advantage of the 1948 legislation, which empowered them to spend money on the arts, gradually, encouraged by the Arts Council, cities and towns subsidised their local repertory company, with some of them, following the example of Coventry's Belgrade Theatre (1958), building new theatres. The number of repertory theatres declined, with many commercial ventures falling victim to the competition of television, but those that survived were now underpinned by public funds.

The repertory movement had long advocated the founding of a National Theatre and at last the climate was right.

The National Theatre and the Royal Shakespeare Company

The recognition of the state's responsibility for its culture engendered during the Second World War, the example of other European nations, the excitement of the 1950s new wave and the prospect of celebrating Shakespeare's quatercentenary (in 1964) all conspired to bring about the long-awaited National Theatre, which was established at the Old Vic under the leadership of Laurence Olivier in 1963. However, Stratford had stolen a march on the capital with its new artistic director Peter Hall, who had succeeded **Glen Byam Shaw** (1904–1986) in 1960, convincing (first) his chairman **Sir Fordham Flower** (1904–66) and other key figures that the Memorial Theatre should be transformed into a national company on continental lines. In 1961 the company was renamed the Royal Shakespeare Company and Hall's ambitious plans were underway.

The main planks of Hall's policy were: a semi-permanent acting company with two- to three-year contracts; a London theatre; a contemporary approach to Shakespeare; the development of a house style in acting and design; an experimental studio and the encouragement of new writing. With Hall sharing its direction with **Peter Brook** and **Michel Saint-Denis**, the RSC was a 'directors' theatre. Brook's *King Lear* (1962) with **Paul Scofield** (1922–) *Marat/Sade* by Peter Weiss and the documentary *US* (1966) – levelled at the United States's entanglement in Vietnam – exposed audiences to the ideas of Artaud and Brecht permeated through Brook's own distinctive talent. Nevertheless during its early years the RSC assembled an outstanding acting company with the experience of **Peggy Ashcroft** and **John Gielgud**, **Dorothy Tutin** (1931–) and **Judi Dench** (1934–) whose promise was already recognized, and newcomers **Diana Rigg** (1938–), **Glenda Jackson** (1936–), **Ian Richardson** (1934–) and many more besides.

Even as it withdrew from negotiations about becoming part of the nascent National Theatre ('competition is healthier than monopoly' proclaimed Sir Fordham Flower) the RSC was complaining about inequitable Arts Council funding (£40,000 to £130,000) as it has continued to do ever since. Whether a merger of the RSC and the National would have worked will never be known. Clearly the two institutions had much in common – the European model of a state theatre – but the appointment of Laurence Olivier as the first Artistic Director of the National Theatre signalled that it was going to be more of an actors' theatre as did his opening production: *Hamlet* (22 October 1963) with **Peter O'Toole** (1932–) as the Prince, **Michael Redgrave** (1908–85) as Claudius, **Diana Wynyard** (1906–64) as Gertrude and **Rosemary Harris** (1930–) as Ophelia. The presence of Kenneth Tynan as literary manager ensured a European dimension not just with the choice of plays (Chekhov, Ibsen, Frisch and Brecht), but also guest directors such as **Jacques Charon** for **John Mortimer**'s (1923–) translation of Feydeau's *A Flea in the Ear*, 1966; **Franco Zeffirelli** (1923–) for *Much Ado About Nothing* in 1965 and the Berliner Ensemble's **Manfred Wekwerth** (1929–) for *Coriolanus* in 1971. The Berliner Ensemble visited in 1965, a complement to the RSC's annual World Theatre Season. **Peter Shaffer** (1926–) with *The Royal Hunt of the Sun* in 1965, **John Arden** with *Armstrong's Last Good Night*, also 1965, and **Tom Stoppard** (1937–) with *Rosencrantz and Guildenstern are Dead* in 1967 provided plays on a scale worthy of the new venture. From 1968, following the abolition of the Lord Chamberlain's role as licenser of plays, they were no longer subject to censorship.

However, it was the performances, by **Joan Plowright** (1929–), **Michael Redgrave**, **Albert Finney**, **Maggie Smith** (1934–) and **Edith Evans** – to name but a few – which were the glories of the National's early years.

Laurence Olivier

As befitted the consummate actor, Olivier seemed to embody every change which the theatre underwent during his career. He began in repertory in Birmingham in 1926; savoured West End and Broadway success in Coward's *Private Lives* 1930; shared the honours (alternating Romeo and Mercutio) in Gielgud's *Romeo and Juliet* (1935); joined the Old Vic (1937) and became a Hollywood star (1939). There was continuity nevertheless; Hollywood gave him the experience of cinema to make his Shakespeare films (*Henry V* 1944, *Hamlet* 1947, *Richard III* 1954) and he returned to the Old Vic as Artistic Director with **Ralph Richardson** (1902–83) during 1944–9. In the early 1950s he ran his own management in the West End, in 1955 he led the star-studded season at Stratford, but in 1958 he was an eager recruit to the new wave as Archie Rice in Osborne's

The Entertainer. In 1962 he opened the Chichester Festival Theatre which, with its bold thrust-stage, provided something of a curtain-raiser for the National the next year.

Though afflicted with ill-health Olivier added to his laurels at the National Theatre, especially as an actor, with Shylock in 1970, and – his last stage role – Tagg in **Trevor Griffiths**'s (1935–) *The Party* in 1973, but the circumstances in which he was succeeded by Peter Hall in 1973 were deeply upsetting for him. Knighted in 1947 Olivier was created Baron Olivier of Brighton in 1970. He was married three times: Jill Esmond, **Vivien Leigh** (1913–67) and Joan Plowright.

The Olivier Theatre at the National Theatre, London, 1976

Mixed economy

The appointment of Peter Hall, who had resigned from Stratford in 1968, as Olivier's successor raised questions about how different the National was from the RSC. As artistic director of the RSC Hall had formulated the key concepts for the Company's London home at the Barbican into which it finally moved in 1982. In the meantime he led the National's gradual occupation (1976–7) of Denys Lasdun's complex on the South Bank comprising the large open-stage Olivier, the proscenium-arch Lyttleton and the chamber Cottesloe. In 1997 **Richard Eyre** (1943–) who had succeeded Hall in 1986 was himself succeeded by the RSC's former artistic director (1968–86) **Trevor Nunn** (1940–). The pool of talent equal to the standards required by national companies being limited, the same actors, directors and dramatists find themselves in demand at both the NT (Royal from 1988) and RSC. Ironically it is the RSC, whose erstwhile chairman Sir Fordham Flower upheld competition over monopoly, that has suffered most in this contest with its artistic director **Adrian Noble** (1950–) withdrawing the company from the Barbican for half the year.

This change in policy was occasioned partly by the opening of 'Shakespeare's Globe Theatre' for its first full season in 1997, the realization of **Sam Wanamaker**'s (1919–93) ambition to build a reconstruction of the Globe Theatre as near as possible to its original site.

The Globe Theatre, London, during a performance of Henry V

That the challenge of creating the Globe Theatre in London should be undertaken by an American actor born to Russian Jewish emigres in Chicago is a vivid illustration of the truly international nature of theatre in the late twentieth century.

The Globe was financed by persistent private fund-raising around the world over many years. In contrast, during the later 1990s, many theatres in Britain received (and many more applied for) National Lottery awards to finance improvements and additions to their premises.

The existence of a mixed economy in the theatre is clearly vital to its health in the closing years of the second millennium. Actors such as Judi Dench, Diana Rigg, **Nigel Hawthorne** (1939–) and **Donald Sinden** (1923–) move easily between the commercial and subsidized sector; the plays of Tom Stoppard, **Alan Ayckbourn** (1939–) and **David Hare** (1947–) transfer from – in Ayckbourn's case – Scarborough to the National, RSC or West End and then back to regional theatres. Trevor Nunn, as well as being past and present artistic director of the two national companies, has achieved huge successes in the commercial musical theatre as director of **Andrew Lloyd Webber**'s (1948–) *Cats* (1981) and *Starlight Express* (1984) and **Cameron Mackintosh**'s (1946–) long-running *Les Miserables* (1985) which originated with the RSC. In 1998 Nunn's National revival of Rodgers and Hammerstein's *Oklahoma* (1943) was supported by a 'generous donation from the Mackintosh Foundation'. International film-stars such as **Juliette Binoche** and **Nicole Kidman** readily appear at basic rates for prestigious fringe theatres such as the Almeida and the Donmar in London.

The position which is often claimed for Britain as the theatrical centre of the world rests upon many factors: its own remarkable tradition; the continuing supremacy of Shakespeare; its proximity to, and wariness of, Europe; its language – shared with the United States – achieving international primacy and much besides. Now, as throughout its history, the theatre is a magnet and a means for ideas and individuals to cross barriers and borders.

RECOMMENDED READING

General

Banham, Martin ed. *The Cambridge Guide to World Theatre*, Cambridge University Press, 1988, rev. 1995

Hartnoll, Phyllis ed. *The Oxford Companion to the Theatre*, Oxford University Press, 1965

Hodgson, Terry, *The Batsford Dictionary of Drama*, Batsford, 1988

Leacroft, Richard, *The Development of the English Playhouse*, Eyre Methuen, 1973

Nagler, A.M. *A Source Book in Theatrical History*, Dover, 1952

Rosenfeld, Sybil, *A Short History of Scenic Design in Great Britain*, Blackwell, 1973

Southern, Richard, *The Seven Ages of the Theatre*, Faber and Faber, 1964

Classical – Greek and Roman – (Chapter 1)

Beacham, Richard C. *The Roman Theatre and Its Audience*, Routledge, 1991

Bieber, Margarete, *The History of the Greek and Roman Theatre*, Princeton University Press, 1961

Easterling, P. E. *The Cambridge Companion to Greek Tragedy*, Cambridge University Press, 1997

Medieval Theatre (Chapter 2)

Beadle, Richard, ed. *The Cambridge Companion to Medieval English Theatre*, Cambridge University Press, 1994

Butterworth, Philip, *Theatre of Fire – Special Effects in Early English and Scottish Theatre*, The Society for Theatre Research, 1998

Wickham, Glynne, *The Medieval Theatre*, Weidenfield and Nicolson, 1980

Tudor England (Chapter 3)

Gurr, Andrew, *The Shakespeare Stage 1574–1642*, Cambridge University Press, 1995
Playgoing in Shakespeare's London, Cambridge University Press, 1996

Mulryne, J. R. and Shewring, Margaret eds. *Shakespeare's Globe Rebuilt*, Cambridge University Press in association with Mulryne and Shewring, 1997

Thomson, Peter, *Shakespeare's Professional Career*, Cambridge University Press, 1994

Wells, Stanley ed. *The Cambridge Companion to Shakespeare Studies*, Cambridge University Press, 1996

New Perspectives (Chapter 4)

Mulryne, J. R. and Shewring, Margaret eds. *The Theatre of the English and Italian Renaissance*, Macmillan, 1991

Orrell, John, *The Theatres of Inigo Jones and John Webb*, Cambridge University Press, 1985
The Human Stage. English theatre design 1567–1640, Macmillan, 1988

Restoration Theatre (Chapter 5)

Powell, Jocelyn, *Restoration Theatre Production*, Routledge, 1984

Muir, Kenneth, *The Comedy of Manners*, Hutchinson, 1970

Thomas, David ed. *Theatre in Europe: a document history. Restoration and Georgian England 1660–1788*. Cambridge University Press, 1989

The Eighteenth Century (Chapter 6)

Donohue, Joseph, *Theatre in the Age of Kean*, Blackwell, 1975

Price, Cecil, *Theatre in the Age of Garrick*, Blackwell, 1973

West, Shearer, *The Image of the Actor. Verbal and Visual Representation in the Age of Garrick and Kemble*, Pinter, 1991

Victorian Theatre (Chapter 7)

Booth, Michael, *Theatre in the Victorian Age*, Cambridge University Press, 1991

Foulkes, Richard, *Church and Stage in Victorian England*, Cambridge University Press, 1997

Jackson, Russell ed. *Victorian Theatre – a New Mermaid Background Book*, A & C Black, 1997

Rowell, George, *The Victorian Theatre*, Clarendon Press, 1956

Europe (Chapter 8)

Braun, Edward, *The Director and the Stage from Naturalism to Grotowski*, Methuen, 1982

Brockett, Oscar G. and Findlay, Robert R. *Century of Innovation: A History of European and American Theatre and Drama Since 1970*, Prentice Hall, 1973

Innes, Christopher, *Avant Garde Theatre 1892–1992*, Routledge, 1993

Twentieth Century (Chapter 9)

As for Chapter 8 and:

Beauman, Sally, *The Royal Shakespeare Company A History of Ten Decades*, Oxford University Press, 1982

Day, Barry, *This Wooden 'O' Shakespeare's Globe Reborn*, Oberon Books, 1997

Elsom, John and Tomalin, Nicholas, *The History of the National Theatre*, Jonathan Cape, 1978

INDEX

ty TEACH YOURSELF

ACTING

Ellis Jones

Does the world of acting hold an irresistible pull for you?

What are the essential 'nuts and bolts' of the craft, whether you're an aspiring amateur or professional?

How do you find out if you're good enough to succeed as a professional in the theatre and/or on screen?

What is the most useful form of training – drama school or university?

Do you need to join Equity, and if so how do you go about it?

These and lots more questions concerned with this sometimes glamorous, sometimes heartbreaking art form are addressed in this book by the Vice-Principal of RADA, one of the world's most famous acting schools.

Ellis Jones is a professional director, writer and actor. His productions have ranged from *Macbeth* to *Uncle Vanya* and include many Ayckbourn comedies. Scripts include original plays and adaptations, and performances range from the Fool in *King Lear* to resident characters in two TV sitcoms.

ty TEACH YOURSELF

HOW TO WRITE
A PLAY

David Carter

Teach Yourself How to Write a Play is both an invaluable introduction for the beginner looking to shape and structure their ideas, and an incisive analytical tool for the more experienced writer wanting to refine aspects of their writing. Through the use of practical exercises David Carter takes the aspiring playwright through the vital stages needed to translate an idea into a finished play.

The book:

- covers the writing of stage, film, TV and radio plays
- includes exercises for use with either undeveloped ideas, finished plays or favourite plays
- is as relevant to the beginner as to writers looking to improve or reshape completed plays.

David Carter is a trained actor and experienced writer and director. He is also founding member of TRESPASS, a Cambridge company dedicated to the promotion of new writing.

Other related titles

 TEACH YOURSELF

CULTURAL STUDIES

Will Brooker

Teach Yourself Cultural Studies provides a comprehensive introduction to this popular and exciting subject. The key theorists and issues are discussed in a lively and easy-to-follow style – suitable for both beginners and first-level students.

The book:

- introduces and explains Cultural Studies from its historical origins to recent work on video games, TV fandom and the internet
- summarises, examines and critiques the work of key theorists
- communicates complex ideas in a clear and concise way.

Will Brooker has lectured in Media, Film and Communication Studies and is currently researching and teaching at the University of Wales, Cardiff.

Other related titles

MEDIA STUDIES

Brenda Downes and Steve Miller

What is Media Studies? Why has it become the fastest growing subject area in post-16 education? How can our own experiences and knowledge of the media help us when studying them?

This book provides a clear introduction for those embarking·on a course of study and for those who wish to have an overview of current debates about the media.

Teach Yourself Media Studies

- ■ explains concepts used in Media Studies
- ■ introduces essential knowledge for 16+ examinations
- ■ discusses issues central to the study of the media
- ■ uses examples across a range of media technologies
- ■ suggests relevant practical activities
- ■ offers a guide to further study.

The authors have a wide experience of teaching media through all age ranges up to and including graduate and post-graduate level, and are currently producing educational material in a variety of media.